My Dad, Al "Huck" Fenn, used to eat onions like you would an apple. He adored my Ailsa Craigs. My Mom, Beverly Fenn, was excited to hear me read parts of this book and to see all the flowers, fruit and vegetables in person and via Face Time. She was my loving and loved supporter.

So, here it is. This book is dedicated to you both, Huck and Bev. You live on in my memories and in the soil I turn, the air I feel on my cheek, the flower I pick and in the onion I chomp upon.

CONTENTS

A MAINE GARDEN ALMANAC

Seasonal Wisdom for Making the Most of Your Garden Space

MARTHA FENN KING

Down East Books
MAINE

Down East Books
Published by Down East Books
An imprint of Globe Pequot
Trade division of The Rowman & Littlefield Publishing Group, Inc.
4501 Forbes Blvd., Ste. 200
Lanham, MD 20706
www.rowman.com
www.downeastbooks.com

Distributed by NATIONAL BOOK NETWORK

Interior Design by Lynda Chilton, Chilton Creative

Library of Congress Cataloging-in Publication Data on file

ISBN 978-1-68475-008-5 (paperback)
ISBN 978-1-68475-009-2 (e-book)

∞™ The paper used in this publication meets the minimum requirements of American National Standard for Information Sciences—Permanence of Paper for Printed Library Materials, ANSI/NISO Z39.48-1992.

INTRODUCTION

I was about five years old. My older brother Peter and I were sitting in the lobby of the local hospital. My parents were visiting a friend and children were not allowed to visit back then. We quietly sat, waited and watched.

And watched I did with so many people arriving and leaving and going about their business. I remember studying the nurses and doctors walking by. Their white coats, dresses and shoes sure stood out. What really struck me was their stride and purposeful gait. They seemed to know where they were going, what they were doing and had an air of confidence. I decided that very hour that I would become a nurse. And so I did.

My Uncle Sam was an editor for the Reader's Digest and he wrote a lot. Long ago, I decided that I would write some day as well. I have been writing all along. I often enjoyed my nursing work, but my soul and spirit were singing a slightly different song.

This song of yearning had to do with the outdoors, gardens, animals, insects and plants. What was very consistent in my life has been a passion for the natural world. Both my parents Bev and Al, gardened: Mom grew the flowers, cherry tomatoes and herbs; Huck the vegetables. I moved to Camphill Village in Copake, NY just before turning 19 which kick started my career working with individuals of all abilities and started my quest to learn to garden well. I vividly remember transplanting leeks into the bountiful Biodynamic garden. The time spent at Camphill has guided me positively in many ways over the years, ways that I can't even articulate and perhaps ways that I am not even aware of. Gardening continued as a main part of my life over the years in West Virginia and now in Maine.

Since being outside and gardening were second nature to me and I wanted to write something I was passionate about, I decided to start a column for the local newspaper, The York Weekly (seacoastonline.org). The writings were about my vegetable and flower gardens. Trials and tribulations of gardening, tips for beginning and seasoned gardeners, healthy benefits of eating particular plants and the showcasing of various fruits, vegetables or flowers were the roots of the column. Why not compile all of this into one colorful book? Why not travel through the life of a Maine garden and gardener in the manner of an almanac? Why not produce a beautiful gift and include poems?

Thus, intent number three came to fruition. I sowed the seeds, nurtured the baby seedlings and now am delightfully harvesting and reaping the rewards due to perseverance and intention. You are holding a book of essays, poems, simple recipes and musings all rolled into one for people of all gardening abilities to enjoy. This book is a gift for gardeners and for others who appreciate nature, for people who respect our earth, for people who want to increase their knowledge base or are seeking some inspiration.

SPRING

1

Buzzing—So Much to Learn from Beehive Activity

Since I was a kid I have liked honeybees. I was never fearful of them and just thought they were really neat. I liked their honey also. My dad taught us to respect bees. I heard him say to not move abruptly and to be calm as they won't sting you. Hearing these words helped instill a near-inherent calmness around the honeybees. It seemed that there were many bees during my childhood..

No honeybees have beeb seen this early Spring. It was the first spring in a few years in which there have been no sightings of honeybees—not on the peach nor pear blossoms nor sour cherry, Lily of the Valley, daffodils nor dandelion. They are missing and I miss them!

It turned out that my neighbor's bees died over the winter apparently from the cold and perhaps compounded from not

having enough food in the hive to sustain them through a long and tough time. Some other native pollinators flew about, including the bumblebee, but it was grossly apparent my little bee friends were absent.

What a nice surprise when my neighbor Pete purchased a hive with a queen and about 6,000 bees. He placed the queen bee encased in a little wire and wood box into the wooden beehive and then he shook the bees from the transport box in there too. Boy, were they buzzing around! They were a tad aggravated, but after a half-hour or so they started settling in. Many of them immediately hovered around the queen while others started exploring their new digs or swarmed around the entrance.

I have read, observed and listened to stories about his other hives. And, wow, bees in general are simply fascinating! There are guard bees at the entrance that keep predator insects out of the hive, and there are bees that dance to let the others know where to get the pollen. If the queen is sick or dying, the other designated bees get a new queen "ready" to take over for her, and some even clean the hive by pushing out debris through the front door.

> **Perhaps more people should stand by a bee hive, observe and contemplate life; we may learn a thing or two about communication, respect, preparation, work ethics, state of world affairs and healthy living. Yes, bees! Yes, food!!**

Over decades and all around the world, bees have died and continue to die in large numbers. Some beekeepers lost 20 to 50 percent of their hives to mites, viruses and colony collapse disorder, which has been linked to neurotoxins and poor bee keeping habits that have been in place for decades. Spikenard Farm Honeybee Farm Sanctuary in Floyd, Va., sums it up: "We believe that the present loss in vitality and reduced capability of survival of the honeybee is not only caused by conventional agricultural practices with their monocultures and poisons, but also by our attempt of making beekeeping as profitable as possible, which has driven and shaped our practices for over 100 years, including:

- ✔ *Artificial queen breeding*
- ✔ *Recycled wax or plastic foundations*
- ✔ *Feeding sugar/corn syrup in large quantities*
- ✔ *Exploitive honey harvests*
- ✔ *Swarm prevention*
- ✔ *Migratory beekeeping*

Spikenard Farm Honeybee Farm Sanctuary, which practices sustainable, natural and biodynamic beekeeping, has had wonderful success with only 5 to 20 percent loss of their hives over 10 years (nationally it has been well over 30 percent loss). In 2014—get ready for this folks—100 percent of Spikenard's 35 hives, with the queens very much alive, survived the long, cold winter! Their bees are getting stronger with healthy and happy immune systems, generation after generation. Check out their website, Spikenardfarm.org, and learn about natural bee keeping; learn what flowers and herbs are important to grow to support the bees—they sell packets of seeds that grow into the flowers that have the pollen that the bees love and need.

So what is all the fuss about bees? The honeybees are the pollinators of our world's crops, such as almonds, apples, cucumbers and broccoli — without them we would not have these delectable, nutritious foods. The bee is a really, really important insect. Oh, and then there is the honey! And the beeswax! And the propolis!

2

So Many Delicious Leafy Choices

Greens, greens, greens! It is springtime and people think about lettuce and perhaps kale as something leafy to munch on, but there are so many possibilities to choose from, which makes it a really great time of year for culinary delights.

Mustard greens, pac choi, cress and arugula are a few "greens" that I have grown in my garden, but have you heard of tatsoi, mizuna, sorrel, micro greens and mache? If you have ventured to any of the farmers markets you may have been introduced to the wide selection that is available. It is fun to walk around and see the variety, color and textures and then buy something new and experiment at home.

Foragers who go into woods or fields or garden to gather food also have a plethora of choices in the spring. I am most familiar with fiddlehead ferns, nettles, morel mushrooms, broad leaf plantain and wild onion. The photo shows a leafy mix. Take a guess—what are you seeing? I sautéed stinging nettles (Urtica dioica), spinach and dandelion greens in several tablespoons of olive oil until wilted, then added sliced shiitake mushrooms and crushed garlic. Then the greens were placed on quinoa and topped with salmon pieces. Voila! Oh yes, the stinging in the stinging nettles gets cooked out and these greens have iron and also silica, which is great for our bones.

I now look forward to the nettles, purslane and dandelion greens in early spring. What floats your culinary boat and how do you prepare your nutritious greens?

You may not be venturing out into the forest to gather your food, but your yard may be able to provide you with "bonus foods" to eat. Get your garden started (tricky this year with cool nights and no rain—just one-fifth of an inch in the last four weeks)—peek around to see if you have purslane or broad leaf plantain or some other edible growing in your neck of the woods. It is fun to explore the outdoors and learn something new about plants, especially now knowing that they are not simply weeds, but potential food sources. So, what is growing in your garden? Please note—If you decide to gather any plant to eat outside of your usual garden veggies, be sure you know what you are doing: consult an "expert" before eating any mushroom or plant from yard, field or forest! Seek out an herbalist or forager.

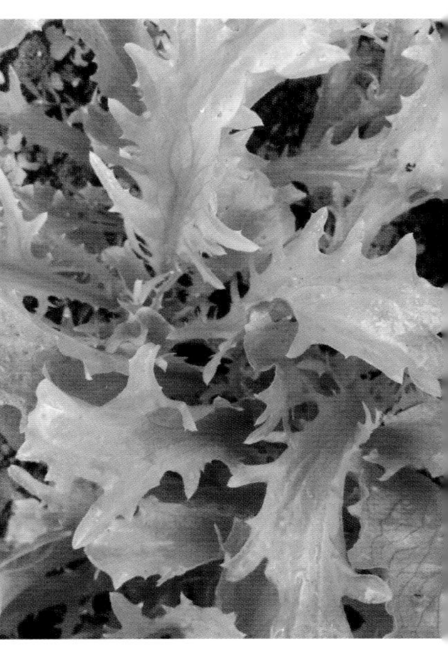

3

Every Day Should Be Earth Day

Earth Day is a day in April to ponder the plight of our "precious and fragile earth." A day to give thanks for the land we live upon, the water we drink and use daily and the air we breath from the moment we leave our mother's womb sustaining us until our last breath. A day to give thanks for the forests and plains and mountains and savannas and gardens and bogs and deserts. This is a day to say thank you for all that we receive from this amazingly diverse planet. All over the world people gather to give thanks and spread messages of hope and ideas for how we each can care for our own little piece of our world.

This is a day to thank people like Rachel Carson for using poetic words as a message to people of the dangerous consequences of spraying poisons on our living earth. For others such as Pete Seeger who not only sang the words of hope and peace, but years ago jumped on the sloop *Clearwater* to help spread the word of just how polluted the majestic Hudson River was. For visionaries or forward thinkers who knew inherently that the ways of this world are not always beneficial for her. For the celebrities, scientists, farmers, gardeners, regular folk who think about our earth on a daily basis.

E. B. White wrote, "I am pessimistic about the human race because it is too ingenious for its own good. Our approach to nature is to beat it into submission. We would stand a better chance of survival if we accommodated ourselves to this planet and viewed it appreciatively instead of skeptically and dictatorially." As people before us gathered food, they used only what they needed. In the 21st century it does appear we have a tendency to plunder and take much more than is necessary. Greed, power and money play hugely into this quota. People say industrial practices are for the greater good of humanity but how can this be if in reality our earth is continually polluted with plastics, pesticides, herbicides and other toxic chemicals in water, air and soil? Garbage is still dumped into waterways. Lawns are being sprayed to kill "weeds." GMO crops are adrift. Chronic illness and disease are ever present. We humans are not sensitive to the needs of our earth. Our Earth is crying out for our assistance.

Take a moment and look at the bees. The numbers have dwindled with hives lost due to colony collapse disorder linked to neonicotinoid sprays (and other reasons) that weaken the bees causing an increase in infestations of mites, disease and death amongst our pollinators and friends, the bees. Yes, our friends. As E.B. White mentioned our dictatorial ways, why then don't we look at our Mother Earth or Partner Earth (Pam Montgomery) as our friend instead of submitting her to such injustices? As friends we could work together to heal. We would be appreciative of one another. The earth would benefit hugely and thus humans would too: at the same time we could heal our wounds of war, terror, disease, fear, negative farming practices and polluting ways.

As a child I lived in the Hudson River Valley in upstate New York. We were surrounded by farms, Holsteins, apple orchards and corn fields. On rainless, still days, a plane would come flying overhead to the nearby orchards, swoop down and unload a mist. When my mother heard that plane, she would holler to me, my friends and siblings to come in the house and close all the windows. My mother must have read about the negative effects of DDT or maybe read something written by Rachel Carson. We were running quite literally for our lives and I thank her for her wisdom. I thank her for her wisdom. Some years hence, I was told the news that the pilot of that plane died of lung cancer. I have to tell you that has stuck with me like burdocks on a wool sweater and I will never, ever forget—was there a link between that spray and the cancer? I have since thought so and that is one reason I am a proponent of sustainable farming and gardening practices, in particular Biodynamics which works with cosmic influences (think moon and effect on ocean tides) and has great respect for beneficial organisms, insects, animals and humans. This is similar to organic gardening and farming that does not use

synthetic pesticides or herbicides that are detrimental to animals, humans, insects and microorganisms –it is a way toward healing.

So on Earth Day let us learn from our past mistakes. Going forward we can make small steps to benefit our friend the bee or our friend the topsoil or our friend the lady beetle or bird or person. Turn our thoughts and practices to healing the earth and in return each other. Every day is Earth Day. May you and I appreciate what we have and make choices that benefit earth, each and every day. I will use less plastic. What might you do? No pesticide spray? Great! Our "precious and fragile" earth and I, thank you.

4
First Produce of the Season

I went to the Portsmouth (NH) Farmers Market and it was truly amazing to see all the beautiful and hardy vegetable, herb and flower plants plus produce that were available for sale. Growers all around New England and beyond are gearing up to move local produce and seedlings from their farms and gardens to your dinner plate. If you have a home garden and are in need of seedlings, there are many vegetable and herb plants to choose from at any given farmer's market or directly from a local farm. If you don't have a home garden there are vegetables to buy, take home and consume. Have fun experimenting with new varieties.

In Martha's Garden the garlic and French shallots that I planted last October are doing well, in part, to the insulation of hefty snow cover and mulch. 0.8 inches of rain fell this past Saturday morning which caused them to grow dramatically, as

you can just about see their growth if you look closely. Although not ready to harvest the mature garlic bulbs until July, small garlic plants can now be eaten like an oniony scallion. Before we know it, the tender, curled scapes or flower stems of the garlic plant will be ready to cut and use in pesto, a veggie medley or even in your chicken soup.

Many people aound here wait until Memorial Day to plant their gardens. It seems as though this is just a tradition, but it may be based more on scientific meteorology or climatology statistics indicating when frosts have historically occurred, which in this case is the third week or so in May. Thus, you don't want to lose your tomato plants to a frost, so having some patience and waiting till late May or even early June may be beneficial in the long run for these heat-loving vegetable plants.

How do all those local farmers have all this produce and plants now, so early in the growing season? Greenhouses are essential as well as hoop houses as the grower is able to get an early start. In my garden I use floating row covers over top of the plants that allows sunlight to filter through, making a mini micro climate that increases the temperature a few degrees and keeps the deer out (other animals too) giving the plants a little boost. Swiss chard, arugula, cress, cutting lettuce, cilantro, spinach and turnips are all growing under this fabric and quite like it. These are all cool-weather plants. Tomatoes, peppers, squash and eggplants are warm-weather plants, those that thrive on warmer temps and do not like it cool or cold. Many home gardeners only plant warm weather veggies; there are tons of cool-weather crops that can be planted (without cover) before the end of May that you may enjoy eating. I have planted so far: peas, potatoes, onions, shallots, beets, kale, lettuce, spinach and carrots. Getting a jump on the garden a tad earlier may benefit you and your family with fresh, nutritious produce by extending the gardening season.

When it comes to eating veggies: don't let your past dictate what you might eat now; try it, you might just like it.

I usually start some of the cool weather plants outside in a "cold frame," which is a wooden box with a glass or plastic cover on top. I call it my "nursery" as many babies are started in the frame and wind up in the garden when ready to be transplanted. This year seedlings were started under the "microclimate row cover" that covers a raised bed. There are little head lettuces, kales, collards, swiss chard, pac choi and broccoli in various stages of growth, which I will pluck out and transplant soon into the main garden. You can see that there are many "early" vegetable choices to try growing in your garden.

Local food remains bountiful even throughout our cold winters with the use of greenhouses, row covers and hoop houses. With a little effort you can produce a plethora of veggies to supplement your diet. So whether you have a little cottage garden or have no garden at all, come to a cold or warm season farmers market and check out what is on the menu for the week.

5

Harvesting Asparagus—Every Day!

Asparagus! We have a four-year-old Asparagus officinalis bed and are harvesting the beautiful stalks nearly every day. We waited until the plants were three years old before cutting to allow the root systems to get established. This spring vegetable, if properly planted and annually fertilized with compost, will produce edible spears for fifteen to twenty years. If anyone out there has an older plot, please let me know.

Asparagus provides vitamin C, A, K, B's and calcium, fiber, magnesium, chromium, beta carotene, etc. It is known as a mild diuretic and due to the inherent glutathione, may even help fight cancer cells, viruses, and bacteria. Glutathione is our "master anti-oxidant" that reduces oxidative stress and those darn free radicals. The delicate, unique flavor of the Asparagus stem is outstanding and any health benefits a huge bonus. You need to harvest before the stems turn into a frilly fern-like 6-foot forest—I happen to love the fern forest and use them in flower bouquets. Usually we cut the stems near the ground or an inch above or so. We wait until they are anywhere from about 5 inches—9 inches and we love the fat, plump stalks which are some times eaten raw.

We had ample rain in April and mixed with sunshine and warmth, the spears broke through the earth and we have been cutting them for several weeks. My favorite method to prepare the asparagus is: wash, trim the cut end a little, toss with olive or avocado oil and chopped garlic (several cloves)—then roast at 400F for about 14 minutes or until fork tender—so excellent! Toss cut-up asparagus into an omelet, scrambled eggs, soup, stir fry or throw the long spears onto the grill. Spring is not spring without the sumptuous asparagus. Enjoy!

I love watching the various stages of all my plant friends. Like the asparagus plant, may you be nourished sufficiently from the roots up and flourish into all that you desire and wish for in your life.

6

Getting Ready to Dig in the Ground

We have so much to learn about life, just from the humus under our feet.

It is still hidden under mounds of snow and has not been seen since early December. What am I talking about? Soil, earth,dirt, humus.

What actually is humus? Humus is what I discovered in the woods of my childhood; what I held in my hands and smelled in the Spring; a soft "wooly" blanket upon the Earth. The scent was subtle, slightly sweet and earthy smelling (of course), dark colored and cool to the hands. All leaves, plant debris, small and large animals were decomposed, turned into this unique soil—the final product after perhaps a couple of decades of change. Not one plant or mammal or insect or rodent could be readily identified in that pile of brown humus. It was the ultimate end product of a complex process of decomposition by anaerobic microorganisms morphing into this organic substance. This is not our compost we

are talking about with pieces of twigs, lemon rind and leaves, but a more finished product that has numerous and surprising beneficial properties.

Here are a few things I learned about humus in a master gardener class some years back and in the years that have followed:

- ✔ *Improves soil structure*
- ✔ *Helps aerate the soil*
- ✔ *Holds water really well*
- ✔ *Loosens clay soil*
- ✔ *Improves soil fertility*
- ✔ *Helps a plant develop healthy roots*
- ✔ *Adds nutrients and microorganisms for healthy soil life*
- ✔ *Warms the surface of the soil in Spring*
- ✔ *May help chelate heavy metals*
- ✔ *Potentially can help with carbon sequestration*

With droughts, heavy rains and toxic metals in our soils, humus may be something we look at very seriously. In "The Gardener's Guide to Better Soil" by Gene Logsdon and the editors of *Organic Gardening and Farming* from the Rodale Press say, "The

ROTOTILLING

I must confess that I make a mess
Of the Earth that's under my feet.
I till and till and tilth is nil
As the tiller makes it neat.
I make a pass and another pass
To smooth and level ground, alas!
I know the fungi, peds and loam
The clay, the sand and silt,
Are crying out without a doubt
"Stop" try another route!

much-admired soil scientist George Scarseth, now deceased, used to tell his students that if man took care of the top seven inches of the earth's crust, just about everything else would take care of itself." Maybe we should take heed and care for and learn from our organic matter—perhaps we will have more nutritious foods to eat, microbes for health and a sponge to soak up the rain. Let us care for our humus and topsoil, our ecosystem and microbiome—the Earth depends on our help.

7

What's Starting to Grow in the Garden

So what is cooking, or better yet, growing in your garden? Not so long ago, there was a pile of snow in my lower garden and now the upper garden is so dry the soil is like dust. Yes, I have even had to water some plants this early to mid Spring! And what plants are these you say?

Growing in Martha's Garden are the usual perennials: daffodils, lovage, Russian sage (barely), daisy, lavender, iris, garlic, shallots, lungwort, violets, oregano, scented geranium and more. What I have directly planted so far: peas, arugula, spinach, cress, cutting lettuce, carrots, a new bed of asparagus, potatoes and cilantro. In order for seed germination the soil needs to stay damp (not soaking and cold), especially for carrot seeds to germinate. Many folks tell me they have tried to grow carrots but have failed—this is most likely because the soil and seed dried out. So spring Tip **No.1:** Keep your row/bed of carrots and other vegetable seeds well watered until germination and than thereafter, being sure the tiny seedlings do not dry out. Once they are big enough then you can cut the apron strings and let mother nature take over (unless, of course, there is a horrendous drought—by all means, water up a storm!).

Patience, good planning, and hard work could be blown away in one storm; pick up the pieces, dust yourself off and resume living and dreaming. We *can* do this!

The arugula, cress and baby lettuce seedlings dry out quickly with the wind and bright sun, so about every two days they have gotten a drink. I like to hand water with a watering can, but also use the hose as well. It was a long winter and spring is finally here even with the low 40s in the morning. This is still early May and I have seen snow after the second week—I hear you groaning and I feel your pain. We don't want that, nor do we want 30 to 40 degrees one day then 80 degrees the next, yikes! Those hot days make it seem as though we can transplant any plant into the garden. **Tip No.2:** Perhaps wait awhile until things, meaning weather, settle down. I want desperately to transplant my onion seedlings (started inside under lights) into the ground—planting guides instruct and experience shows that onions are hardy, but after all, these are babies we are talking about.

Tip No.3: Really, really wait to put out all warm weather plants such as tomatoes, peppers, eggplants, etc. This includes your annual flowers—they do not like cold weather and for all we know there could be a frost and that certainly would wipe out those plants. So, patience, planning, timing and keeping an eye to the sky is where we are right now. Well, an ear to your favorite weather person usually works well too.

8
Knowing When to Plant and When to Transplant

Spring is the time in which gardeners plant little seeds in pots indoors or in a greenhouse exposing tiny seedlings to grow lights or sunlight. The time to jumpstart the growing season and have a multitude of plants on the ready to transplant out into "the garden."

This year with whopping amounts of snow, a long cold winter and cool spring, it is tricky business! Gardening and growing healthy plants depends on varying factors as you know, such as the temperature of the soil and air, nutrients or elements such as nitrogen in the soil, the number of beneficial insects in the garden, amount of compost in the soil and so on. Another factor is that a gardener must have a certain size plant to transplant in the ground at a particular time during the growing season. Many people do not have this worry as they buy seedlings from a local garden center, farm or farmers' market and they follow the verbal or written transplant instructions given them at the time of the sale. Those who start their own seedlings must give some thought to this process of when to sow the seed and when to transplant.

When do I start a particular vegetable or flower to have it grow to a certain size and be transplanted at a certain time?

This year I started onions, leeks and shallots as I have done other years—in early March—as it has worked out pretty well historically. Looking out at the garden on April 10 after a couple inches of snow and seeing the snow pack from the winter blanketing a lot of the garden, I admit it is slightly disheartening. The upper garden that is shallow and gets more sun is visible as the snow has melted—which is most encouraging; that is just where the onion seedlings will be transplanted. With a bit of luck the onion babies will go into the ground pretty much on schedule in May.

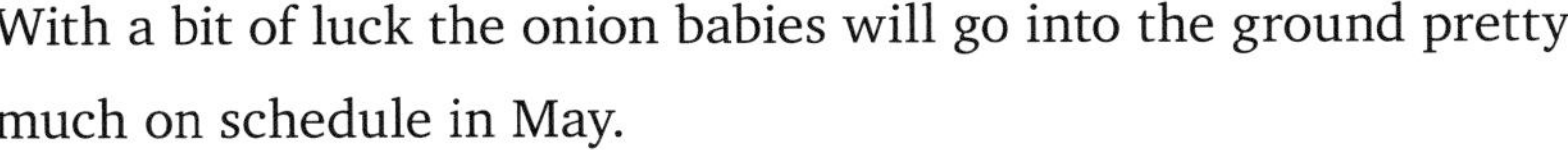

In the Fedco catalog, other seed catalogs and books there will be a planting guide which spells out the ideal temperature for germinating specific seeds, length of time until germination, the time to transplant out into the garden, etc. It really is mainly about timing with a bit of math thrown in. Year after year of starting their own seedlings, some gardeners have a certain sense about it; it becomes second nature to them. Many also keep written records of exactly what they plant and when and refer to the record each year. The gardeners with heated greenhouses can grow the plants to maturity within the greenhouse and other greenhouse growers transplant the seedlings into a field or garden when it is time. Keeping the greenhouse warm enough at night takes energy (gas, wood, solar or oil for example) to keep those little plants warm enough until the outdoor temps settle down (really, that would be settle up!). Please note that some plants can be directly seeded into the soil such as beans, spinach or beets. We are discussing vegetables that need to be started in advance such as tomatoes, peppers and eggplant or flowers such as statice and snapdragons that take many days to mature or produce fruit or flowers.

Just as the sun rises in the East the snow will melt and the garden will dry up a bit and willingly accept the roots of kale, chard and allium. So it will be.

Back to the question about when to plant and when to transplant—let's pick a tomato (cannot wait to do that.) Tomatoes are sensitive to cold, very tender and will not survive a frost; they do not like temps that are 40F or below. So, by a process of elimination, we can easily pick the transplant month—not April since there is snow on the ground and frozen ground; not May because of snow on the ground and frozen ground—just kidding! Typically late May or early June tomatoes are planted in this Zone 4 -5 as the chance for frost will be past. We will see what develops with rain and sun and warmth. Picture it this way: if you start tomato plants in January they may grow really tall and become unwieldy, they may fall over and break or become deficient in nutrients by the time you are able to transplant out into the garden in very early June. Wait a few months to sow the seeds indoors. Check the seed catalogs or the seed packets as they will describe in detail when to plant with the best bet being February through early April—the average for starting the tomato seeds indoors or in the greenhouse. Taking in consideration our cold spring 2015 and other cold springs hence forth, starting seeds in April may work out very well this year. The rate of growth of each tomato plant does depend on the temperature in your house at night and day, available light from your grow lights or windowsill sun and nutritional value of the starter mix. You don't want the starter mix to be too rich at this stage of development. So check the catalogs and seed packets for the info needed to pick your date for starting your other plants. If you have a greenhouse then you are golden and can sow your seeds way early.

Good luck with your starts. Hopefully we will be able to transplant our seedlings into our gardens at just the prime time. May we have sun and warmth and rain to wash away the fog, snow, ice and frozen tundra.

9

It's Early but the Growing Has Begun

It may be spring in Maine, but there are still many chilly days and nights to come. Despite the cold, plants such as daffodils are showing signs of life with beautiful blooms.

Hardy chives are one of the earliest garden plants to peek through the earth. They are delicious chopped fresh in a salad or thrown in a stir fry. The chive blossoms are spicy and can be added to salads, soups, other dishes or made into an herb vinaigrette.

Winter savory can be added to soups, stews or a bean dish, or make a tea with it to drink or gargle with for sore throats.

The quintessential plant of Maine—the lupine! I can't wait to see if this one is blue or red this year.

Planted in October, the dancing garlics poked through the salt marsh hay and will provide all the garlic bulbs a person could wish for.

Cold frames are great for getting a bit of a jump on the growing season as there is a lid to keep the cold out. The sun shines through the plastic or glass and warms the soil and air just as a greenhouse does. Growing are cutting lettuce, arugula and cress.

There are Chinese cabbages growing in the cold frame. They will be transplanted out into the main garden once it is dry and warm enough.

Those little poppy plants that you aren't sure about may mature into a beauty such as these!

French Gray Shallots planted last autumn. Once mature, there could be fifteen bulbs from each plant that will keep for a number of months. Some will be replanted in the garden this fall for next year's harvest.

The blueberry bushes are budding and blossoming. Besides garden cleanup, the blueberries need some compost and either wood chips or pine needles strewn around the shrubs for a mulch. They grow well in an acidic soil so a little sulfur may be needed.

10

Plants Are Growing, All It Took was Sunshine

I believe that there were several drier and warmer days in March than in April and May. This growing season has been damp with cool nights—down to around 39 F near the ocean. About a week ago, there was even a light frost on the low-lying areas of my garden. Seven years ago was the last frost I remember occurring during the month of May.

The full moon is past and the annual flowers and sun-loving vegetables are just now hardening off on the deck. When the plants come out to get "hardened off", they are covered with a screen to prevent sunburn, wilting and death. Hopefully there will be no more frosts until Autumn. When the temperatures dip down at night the warm weather plants are lugged back into the house so they don't get nipped by the cold. These plants include tomatoes, peppers and a wide variety of cutting flowers such as marigold, salvia and Lisianthus. The direct sunshine makes a huge difference in the growth of the plants. The plants on the deck look so healthy and happy and the lettuce transplants in the garden that pretty much just sat there, really hit their stride with abundant sun.

All seasons have challenges with little sun or too much rain. Hopefully, with abundant encouragement, may our gardens of life be prolific filled with light and joy. Happy, sun-filled Spring to you and your garden!

The perennial flower beds have liked the rain and dampness and the daffodils certainly loved it! The daffs appear to be perpetually blooming due to these cool days; violets and Lily of the Valley are spreading and blooming like wildfire. The peonies are reaching for the sky with many buds. What else in the garden is thriving? The rhubarb is tall with gorgeous leaves. The garlic plants have strong, thick stems. We are eating two varieties of asparagus on a daily basis. One is "Purple Passion" which is so pretty nestled in the straw and hay. The chives, blueberries, raspberries and some herbs seem to be thriving as well.

Unfortunately, some plants took a hit in the winter. Winter kill affected some of the old lavender, lambs ear, culinary sage and possibly the Russian sage plant. This old, large stemmed beauty seemed to be afraid to start sending out new growth. It appeared dead or dormant. With daily verbal conversations and tapping of the woody stems, she has new spring growth. She was just taking her sweet time to awaken from the dark, cold winter.

11

Seeds Have Sprouted; Now What?

And they sure did. The seeds germinated. The little onion and shallot seedlings emerged from the darkness into the light about six days after I planted them. Every year I am thoroughly amazed and delighted to see this new life: a little water, some heat, and voila!

Let's discuss some tips for keeping the seedlings alive until it's time to transplant them into the garden. So, after planting, I placed the onion and shallot containers in the warm furnace room. I checked daily for any signs of life, and on Day 6, I saw the tiny green plants peeping up through the potting soil. Days 7 and 8, I whipped the plastic and rubber bands off the pots to get air circulating and moved them out of the furnace room and under the grow lights. Leaving the plastic cover on the pot would keep the soil too damp and might increase the risk of a fungus developing.

I have my growing stand in my dining room (yes, my family roll their eyes and sigh) next to a big window with hanging full-spectrum or cool-white fluorescent bulbs or lights, also known as "shop lights." Natural light is best for seed starting but these bulbs are similar to sunlight and don't give off too much heat. I hang the long light from chains and lower it to about 2 inches above the newly birthed onion seedlings. With some tiny seedlings like lisianthus, lights have even been closer for a short time. I lift the lights higher as the seedlings grow taller, about 3 inches above the plants. I leave the lights on for about fourteen hours and then the remaining eight hours are dark for the babies. I use a timer to turn the lights on and off when I have several rows of containers of seedlings on the growing stand and things are in full swing. Watering takes place once or twice per week.

Even with yet another storm on the horizon, gardeners here and there are planting, preparing for a healthy, happy, gratifying growing season with "all things" in balance — not too cold, not too hot, not too wet, not too dry. May it be so!

If seedlings don't get enough light, they will get tall and leggy and may become weak, so adequate light and regular watering is a must! I let the potting soil get a bit dry on the top before watering as to not overwater and drown the plants and set up an environment for a mold/fungus to grow. My potting mix has sufficient nutritional supplements to carry the seedlings all the way to when they are transplanted, which can be nearly two months for the onions. So, good luck with your seed starting this season!

12

The First Signs of Spring Have Appeared

Lately I was thinking about my childhood and in particular what I remembered as the first signs of spring—the chives poking through the earth, the creek raging and the invigorating smells. That wonderful season of newness and fresh beginnings—I think it is finally here to stay, although in Maine I have seen snow in May and of course there is a good chance of a few more frosts (sorry!).

It has been a bit of a hard start for some orchardists in New England due to warm days early on that brought the peach and apple buds to swell followed by temperatures dipping down to 15F—zapping those same flowers, which of course means no fruit. I hope the crops of apples and other fruit trees further north are healthy and will be bountiful.

In my garden the cold touched the garlic—the wet snow in combo with the shredded leaf and straw mulch and cold temps

made for some messy looking garlic leaves. Some perennial flowers, such as lilies and even the rhubarb leaves, looked burned or frost bitten.

With some rain and warm weather, everything seems to be growing and blooming and holding its own nevertheless. Oh yes, that one garlic bed I was fretting about in the late fall, it is the best looking of all the garlic! Nature has a way of working things out.

A CACOPHONY CHOIR

A cacophony of birds sound from the moment the
sun peeps over the ocean to the very end of day,
as they settle in their roosts.
Engulfing the garden and the gardener all the day
long are insects, animals, and plants
performing their marvelous interconnected work.
As each sings a different note producing a
marvelous springy chorus of sound and sight,
we humans go about our serious business of living.
Take several moments a day to shift the cadence of
your life—dance with the cacophony choir!

My father enjoyed sharing his knowledge of the natural world with anyone who could listen. His signs of spring have been echoing lately in my mind as the earth is warming. In upstate New York, he would say spring was here to stay when you saw the red-winged blackbird, when the asparagus was pushing through the ground and when the shad were heading up the Hudson to spawn. At this time the Shadbush are in bloom and the Dutchman's Britches too. Fiddle head ferns, wild onions and limey green, baby skunk cabbage are escaping winter's grip. I still remember the smell of the woods and creek that meandered through our property and the smell of shad roe in the skillet. It was a magical time and place.

Take a moment to smell, taste, see, hear, and touch the natural world—you might just be in a proprioception paradise.

In West Virginia, eating spring ramps, which are wild, garlicky, oniony leeks with lily-of-the valley leaves, is, well, a bit of heaven on earth. Spring signs in York, Maine, that I talk about every year are of course the peepers, which are small "chorus frogs" that hang out in or near the pond behind the house. The cacophony of the males is a welcome sound that heralds the change of the dark season into light. After a long cold winter the warming of the earth sends out a distinct "earthy" smell that I always equate with the onset of this much desired season. Our senses—sight, taste, smell and hearing—are in full alertness and our sense of touch is as well. When you pick up handfuls of soil and plant peas—well, that is surely time to call what we are experiencing *Spring*!

SUMMER

13

Pretty, Practical and Prolific— That's Calendula!

Besides growing numerous varieties of vegetables, Martha's Garden also grows numerous flowers—all an important part of the unique micro-climatic ecosystem. Flowers are pleasing to the eye, but perhaps more importantly, they are pleasing to the mind and spirit. They lift our hearts when we are downtrodden and brighten our spirits when we most need it. Each flower is unique with various qualities. The orange flower in the photo is Calendula or Pot Marigold (*Calendula officinalis*), which is a well-known medicinal herb/flower. The orange petals are made into a salve or ointment to treat topical skin problems such as cuts, inflamed skin, burns or fungal conditions. Calendula has many other properties (digestive and detoxifying) and looks simply beautiful in the garden.

The yellow, orange or peachy colored petals are used in place of saffron, as a yellow dye for wool and a compress for bee stings. It's a happy plant and reseeds each year spreading new life amongst the blueberries and asparagus and nearly anywhere it wants to.

14

Any Super Foods in Your Garden?

The following "super" vegetables are growing in Martha's Garden right now: chard, spinach and kale. I would like to focus on two other veggies that may not get as much attention: collards and parsley.

You can obtain your vitamin A and K, some calcium and folate from this Brassica family member—collards. Healthy for your immune system and for strengthening bones, these southern delights are hefty, leafy and green. Due to a thicker leaf they will need more steaming or simmering, but are delectable with some Celtic salt and bacon fat. My husband, Steve, lived in New Orleans and likes to cook collard greens the southern way—boil the heck out of them with pork fat back or ham hock and sometimes onions. I do mean simmer or boil for what is several hours. I suggest steaming them for about 5 minutes. Take a nibble to see if the leaf is tender enough for your liking. If not, steam it some more to tenderize the leaves. Then toss with extra virgin olive oil, a few pinches of sea salt and crushed garlic.

Here's to eating a healthy diet. Let's be successful and experiment out of our comfort zone just a wee bit. Perhaps eat some garlic and then a bouquet of parsley to cleanse your palate.

Next in the garden is parsley, a Mediterranean herb from the Greek word petroselinon, meaning rock celery. *Petroselinum crispum* is the Latin name for both the curly and flat leaf Italian parsley. Both are beautiful with a slightly different green hue. Parsley often gets thrown on a plate as a garnish in restaurants, but I like to make it more center stage on my plate. Parsley can be a major part of your salads, added to tabouli/tabbouleh the Middle Eastern dish, scrambled eggs and soup—you name it! It adds color, some fiber to aid digestion, vitamins C and K, potassium and also lutein and zeaxanthin. I pick a stem or two and nibble away right out of the garden. Eating parsley may keep your immune system strong, your eyes free from developing macular degeneration and may help strengthen your bones. Sounds like a winner to me! The flavor of parsley mellows with cooking but the raw leaves are quite flavorful—many people think the Italian flat leaf is superior to the curled variety, but I like both of them. Sometimes there is a slight bitter flavor or earthiness which I like more and more these days. Parsley that has wintered over has a sweetness that is surprising. Everyday can be soup day and adding a big handful of parsley to your chicken or squash soup may brighten your outlook on life, quite literally.

15

Eat Kale, Then Exhale

Cool weather is upon us so what better veggie to showcase than kale!

My eye doc says "eat greens." Why eat kale? Benefits are that the plant is low in calories but high in Vitamin K, betacarotene, Vitamin C, calcium and contains lutein and zeaxanthin, which are carotenoids that help keep eyes healthy and may prevent macular degeneration. Another component is sulforaphane which may be a potential anti-cancer fighter. So for good eye, bone, and immune health, eat some kale.

Kale is easy to grow, loves cool and even cold weather, tastes better after hit with a frost and can be easy to prepare. Kale seeds can be started inside or out and can be direct seeded or transplanted. "Red Russian" kale with flat, tender leaves, is found in some greens mixes and is cut when very young. Other varieties

of kale such as “Winterbor” or “Redbor”, grow on sturdy stems nearly 4.5-feet tall. Each leaf is cut off the plant with many more leaves following its lead, providing many meals over many weeks or months.

This “cabbage without a head” called borecole by the Dutch is a Scottish word derived from coles, which is Greek, or caulis from the Romans. So whether you call the plant kool, cole, borenkool or nonheading cabbage, kale is close to wild cabbage and is officially Brassica oleracea (cephala group). This family includes cruciferous veggies such as brussels sprouts, broccoli, cauliflower, and collard greens, which many of you may already grow or eat on a regular basis.

Borecole may have curled, flat or crinkled leaves. Siberian or Red Russian has flat leaves, and the Italian heirlooms or “Lacinato” are wrinkled and are also called dinosaur kale. There are also Japanese varieties that are ornamental or decorative with lovely colors. The edible varieties are generally red, purple, or green. I love the way the plants look in the garden with the beautiful colors and statuesque postures!

Beauty is all around us, take a deep breath; look to your right and to your left, look up and down; observe the majestic kale or flower growing in the garden; see the praying mantis climbing the deck, listen to the wind whispering. Exhale and, if you will, eat kale.

Have you heard of Portuguese soup or Caldo verde? Well, yup, there is kale in this soup along with the sausage. There are many exciting ways to use borecole such as tossing a handful into a veggie stir fry or making kale chips. For a quick veggie dish I pick the kale leaves, wash and tear the leaves from the stem. Sauté extra virgin olive or avocado oil (or any fat or oil you choose) in a good size pan with chopped up or crushed garlic—usually one to two cloves from my garden. Next, throw in the kale leaves, simmer until wilted. Toss with fresh squeezed lemon juice, balsamic or red wine vinegar or just leave plain. Sprinkle a little sea salt and enjoy. Don't give up on kale as the various kinds have different flavors and textures and you might just find one you like.

Please note that individuals who are on anticoagulants such as warfarin also known as coumadin and those sensitive to oxalates, may need to consult their health provider before consuming kale.

16
Fennel is Pungent!

What is fennel? Someone at the farmers market asked me that question recently. I described a plant with a licorice smell, kind of like anise. Fennel is member of the Apiacae or Umbelliferae family along with parsley, parsnip, carrot and celery. This herb originates from the coastal areas of the Mediterranean. Culinary fennel has ferny greens atop sturdy, tall stems and a bulbous light green bottom that grows above the ground.

In a nutshell, the Fedco seed catalog states this about fennel: "Genus gets its name from the Latin word for hay, referring to the smell of the foliage, perennial grown as an annual with a licoricey taste. Tender stalks and leaves are good for relishes, salads, and garden munches; leaves and seeds excellent with fish. Seeds used in sweets, baked goods & beverages. Bread becomes impregnated with a faint licorice scent when seasoned with fennel. Fennel

prefers rich well-drained slightly limey soil. Direct seed in late April or early May, do not allow to dry out."

Well, there is more! Fennel goes great with pork tenderloin and chicken, as well as potatoes, green beans, oranges and olives. Fennel is beautiful growing in the garden with the ferny tops dancing in the breeze.

To produce healthy, large bulbs, go ahead and give it a large dose of compost, some water and plenty of sunlight. Fennel can be planted in July and August and will produce mature plants in September into October. Seedlings can actually be transplanted out into the garden, not only direct seeded. With a bit of weed control and watering during a dry spell, or perhaps top dressing with compost, you will harvest some nice looking fennel plants.

When inhaling a handful of the dill-like green foliage, I do smell a faint scent of hay but more of a licorice or anise scent. An Italian friend is wild over finocchio as it grows prolifically in his garden, reseeds and yearly drops its seeds to produce plants the following year.

The umbels or flower heads are lovely and look pretty in flower bouquets. Various publications suggest that fennel seeds have been used for ages to calm digestive problems, increase the milk supply for nursing mothers or as a gargle for sore throats.

Here is a quick recipe to get you started—caramelized fennel, unadulterated. Cut the top and bottom off (save in refrigerator) the whitish bulb and thinly slice the bulbous part of the plant; brown the sliced fennel in a pan with extra virgin olive oil until tender; you can add some butter if you want it browner—don't increase the heat too high; add salt and pepper and squeeze some lemon juice on the fennel, and there you have it. You hopefully will enjoy this veggie dish; try it with a serving of fish and side of roasted sweet or regular potatoes or wild rice.

Enjoy the scents and delicious bounties of the summer!

17
Growing Ginger in the Tropics of Southern Maine

We use this ginger fresh or dried in cookies or cakes, for flavoring stir fries and beverages, and medicinally to treat a bellyache, headache, nausea, vertigo, cough or cold symptoms. I am referring to *Zingiber officinale* rhizomes that grow as roots in the soil and send up narrow leaves that grow off a long stalk-like stem. Ginger usually grows in countries that are frost free such as Jamaica. In India it is known as shringara and the first century A.D. Greeks wrote of zingiberis. It has been traded over the centuries and Spain started cultivating it in the early 16th century. Ginger is a well known and perhaps, the oldest spice; it is especially known for its medicinal properties due to the gingerol, camphene, phellandrene, and zingiberene—chemicals found inherently in the roots.

New England is certainly not Jamaica—or tropical in any way—but ginger cultivation has taken the area by storm. Many market growers (especially those who have greenhouses) have been successful in growing ginger in Maine, Vermont, New Hampshire and New York for a number of years. As a matter of fact, I grew ginger this summer for the first time, right here in York, Maine.

Sunlight, compost, water, soil microbes and nutrients = an environment to grow nearly anything. May your budding projects find nourishment and then multiply into something delightful to palate, belly, mind or soul.

I purchased the ginger rhizomes from Fedco Seeds in Clinton, Maine. They were delivered in March, placed on a tray, covered in dirt, watered once a week and kept in my furnace room until I could get them outside when the weather settled somewhat in late May. I transplanted the roots into the garden and covered them with a low tunnel which, in essence, is metal hoops covered by greenhouse plastic and secured to keep the plastic from blowing away—a mini-greenhouse of sorts. You know that sunlight goes through the clear plastic, which heats the inside making it all cozy and tropical some days. This is sort of like sitting by a window on a cold but sunny day—the solar rays warm the ambient air. With a good amount of compost, some water and heat, the rhizomes multiplied and behold: we harvested juicy, spicy, pink and tan skinned delights that we grate for tea, shred into green meat radish and carrot salads and slice into many vegetable dishes and soups. We love ginger and are so excited about growing our little crop of *Zingiber officinale*. There are many sites to explore online to learn about growing ginger. Try it, and enjoy the challenge. If you have a greenhouse with a heat source besides the sun, you are good to go.

18

Happy Garlic Harvesting—and Eating

I've written about garlic before, but I feel it deserves attention at least annually if not more frequently. Garlic is one of the oldest cultivated plants in the world, originating in western or central Asia and is related to onions and leeks and is in the lily family. Vikings, Romans, and Egyptians ate it for strength. Apparently, vampires don't care for it.

Pliny the Elder, the Roman naturalist supposedly loved it, ate it and popped it in numerous remedies—it turns out that garlic may have anti-viral, anti-fungal or anti-septic properties due in part to the allicin which gives it that stinky odor. There may be other health benefits including improvement in cardiovascular health, healing cold sores, lowering blood pressure, fighting viral infections, etc. I've heard of many anecdotal tales of people eating numerous raw cloves or chugging honey and garlic to ward off colds or the flu. Whether chewing it raw (watch out as it may be spicy and hot!) works for you or not, garlic is still used widely in culinary dishes of all sorts.

Garlicky dishes you may have sampled include: shrimp scampi, pesto, minestrone, garlic tapenade, garlic bread, roasted potatoes, hummus, eggplant ratatouille and homemade Italian pasta sauce. Do you smell a theme here? As you can see, garlic is versatile and can be used in many, many dishes such as Lebanese, Italian and Greek for example. I love it lightly sautéed with olive or avacado oil and tossed with gently steamed swiss chard. The newly dug garlic is sweet and juicy.

> May we not forget the wisdom that has come down through the ages and may we be brave enough to try a new culinary dish or two. See you at the Farmer's Market—Happy summer and happy gardening!

Garlic in my garden is dug in July, each single clove having been planted the previous October. Knowing when to harvest is a tad tricky and takes studying the leaves of the mature plant. If most leaves are dry and brown with just a few at the top of the stem that are still green, then it is most likely time to harvest. I also allow some scapes on the plants to mature into flower heads. If these flower heads are completely straight to the sky I recommend pulling a bulb or two to get a good look at the heads to see if they are mature enough. On a non-rainy day and a good day to work with root crops, I take a garden spading fork and lever the garlic heads out of the earth by gently pulling on the stem as the fork is doing most of the hard work. Try not to stab the garlic! The dirt is knocked or dusted off the bulbs and then the tall, intact stem and bulb and sometimes flower heads are placed horizontally on a screen in the boat house to dry. Harvesting then reaping the juicy, sweet rewards of the hard work of last autumn is very fulfilling—we have a larder piled high with garlic to last until next spring! Happy garlic harvesting and cooking—may your crop be bountiful.

19
Sweet Potato Season Went South

Can you grow sweet potatoes in New England? Yes. Some growers have been quite successful for numerous and consecutive years.

I am not one of them. This season proved to be a bust due to various factors, and my yield was rather pathetic for all the effort and expense put into growing this well-known southern vegetable.

I ordered my slips, or sweet potato plants, during the winter from a farmer in Tennessee. Figuring out at the time of ordering when they should be mailed to Maine was challenging. In the last two years our local weather had been cool and damp when the slips arrived. They are delivered via the postal service. Sweet potatoes like it warm, generally at least 75 degrees. I requested this year for the package to arrive the first week of June. The slips, about 4 to 6 inches in length, are sprouted from the actual roots, sold in groups

of a dozen or more, nicely labeled with the varietal name and held together by a rubber band. Most of the slips have a few leaves on the top, a skinny stem and small, hairy root system. Some of them look half-dead, but, surprisingly, they grow like crazy.

So, what does one do when Mother Nature is not cooperating and it stays too damp and cool to plant the slips? You need to keep the sweet potato slips alive inside the house. I gently separated the bundles of plants and placed each variety in small glass canning jars with the labels attached to identify the sweets. The roots were packed in shredded newspaper so I added a small amount of water at the bottom of the jar so the roots didn't dry out. I kept some of the shredded paper around the roots as well to hold in the moisture.

In the meantime, I prepared the garden by rototilling and building up the beds with compost, so the lengthy roots had room to grow vertically. At the time of planting, I also added a bit more compost, soil amendments (azomite) plus fertilizer (alfalfa meal). Roots love phosphorus so bone char can be added now as well. When it warmed up, I planted the slips about 12 inches apart; rows were about 4 feet apart. I use a large wooden marker and add the date and name of each sweet potato so I can identify them later.

So, what happened this year that caused poor yield? Well, it was a number of factors. My small garden is surrounded by trees that decrease the sunlight each year as they grow taller and taller. My garden shed, maple tree and tall elderberries provided unwanted shade—they will be moved next year. I planted six different varieties, probably too close and the vines were so prolific at about 5 feet in either direction that I believe they added even more shade, thus lowering the soil temperature. The tubers like heat, warm nights, lots of sunlight and water at particular times (at least 1 inch weekly) for optimal root development.

Other problems were of the four-legged variety. The deer loved the vines, so I covered the rows with floating row covers that the deer tore (or hoofed) apart to get at the delectable treats. Then I covered the rows with netting that was used on the blueberries to prevent the birds from devouring the berries. I think that the netting actually cooled down and slowed down the growth of the sweet potatoes. Next year I will let the deer have a nibble of the leaves and not worry so much about the deer damaging the tubers.

Even though there are setbacks in life, such as monstrous vole damage to sweet potato roots, life goes on. Just cut off the gnawed sections and bake the good part; be grateful for even half a potato—and carry on.

Then there were the voles. Yikes! I tried to ignore them, but in the end that was a mistake. As I dug up hill after hill of sweet potatoes, the most mature roots were gnawed upon. It was evident that I will have to resume my previous years' method of trapping voles if I am ever again to have a crop worth keeping for the winter.

Sweet potato tubers — full of complex carbs, dietary fiber, beta-carotene, vitamin C, B6, manganese and potassium — have smooth skin that can be purple, yellow, orange, red or brown. The flesh is white, pink, yellow, red and orange. Some varieties that were previously successful are Beauregard, Vardamon and Georgia Jets. This year I planted some with white and purple flesh but had poor outcomes.

Some of the skins I find edible, but if they are tough, I peel them. Slice or cut the tuber from end-to-end to make spears and place in a bowl. Drizzle extra virgin olive oil or coconut oil, add sea salt, pepper, dried garlic and/or onion powder, dried oregano, a little bit of paprika. You may use fresh herbs, of course. Toss together until all sides of the sweet potatoes are covered. Place on a baking pan at about 450 degrees for 15 to 20 minutes then turn down to about 375 degrees and bake until fork tender. I usually take a spatula and flip them half-way through. Depending on how big they are, the baking time may be about 45 minutes. You will then have delicious "fries."

20
How to Deal with Those Garden Pests—Naturally

With all the tasks involved in growing "vegetable, fruit and flower," it's been a busy late spring and summer for all gardeners. Transplanting, weeding, harvesting and watering during times of drought, for example, all take time. One of the most-time consuming tasks for sustainable, organic and perhaps biodynamic growers may be pest control. So far this year I have seen deer hoof prints and spotted the deer running in the woods behind the garden, cucumber beetles, cutworms, slugs, cabbage moths and, may I dare say (admit), an infestation of aphids on the *Achillea millefolium* or flowering yarrow.

To protect humans, animals, bees, other insects and our dear Mother Earth in general, I absolutely do not use synthetic pesticides or herbicides. Instead, I call in a small army to attack the

May we surround ourselves with all things beneficial. May your garden of life be more or less free of the pests we don't really need so we can focus on positive sowing and growth.

unwanted pests. To help control the aphids, which basically suck the life out of plants, I brought into the garden a horde of lady beetles. They were ravenous and thirsty. The lady bugs started devouring the pesky aphids immediately. For house plants, a little soap or detergent in water sprayed on the plants usually works to control them. I didn't want to harm any beneficial insects with the soap, so I was aimed at experimenting only with the beetles. I first sprayed a little water on the yarrow, and then at the base and inside the cluster of yarrow flowers, I gently dumped the lady bugs out onto the foliage and some on the ground in the cool of the early evening. They walked up the stems and some were placed by hand onto the yarrow stems which had a swarm of aphids attached. The lady beetles immediately started doing their work by eating the aphids and continued to munch on the pests for many a day.

Back in the late spring my neighbor Sharon Trafton received some dragonfly nymphs that we strategically placed in the small pond in the woods behind my house. The nymphs are fascinating to look at in this stage. They are aquatic, molt their "skins" numerous times and are often simply stunning as mature adults with their beautiful colors, aerial stunts and propensity for eating mosquitoes. I have recently seen some mosquito-hawks flying about the garden, and I often wonder and hope that my midwifery skills helped them develop into these lovely beneficial adult insects.

Just recently Sharon kindly brought over a praying mantis egg case. The nymphs were in the process of hatching about 100 to 200 babies. Sharon and her son Jasper helped place the nymphs onto various plants that had some aphids and then spread them out throughout the garden. A praying mantis will grow to about 3 to 4 inches long and will eat just about anything in sight and is even quick enough to grab a mosquito, fly or unfortunately, a butterfly. I am counting on them to devour the aphids and other pests—not the pesty deer of course.

Beneficial insects, such as lady beetle and praying mantis, can be bought at local garden centers or purchased on-line usually in late spring. They come in small plastic containers with holes in the lid for air circulation. Hand picking insects, squishing non-beneficial insect eggs, covering crops with floating row covers and planting flowers, such as marigolds and nasturtiums, and herbs, such as mint, rosemary and sage, all help repel the troublesome insects and attract the helpful ones.

21

Quite a Challenge to Grow in Various Locales

The past two growing seasons found me digging in dirt, not writing. Recently I have expanded gardening hours and decreased my nursing hours. When the cold weather arrives once again, I will do the opposite and work more hours as a developmental disabilities nurse. For now, I am working in four different gardens: the home garden, the Cape Neddick garden and two First Hill gardens.

Last year I "installed" a new garden at the First Hill restaurant on Route 1 just south of York Corner Gardens. In the First Hill garden was a mix of annual flowers, perennials and vegetables. The plants went crazy in the compost and grew like weeds. There were ornamental corn and sunflowers growing together, "Sungold" cherry tomatoes, blueberries, herbs, peppers, potatoes, cucumbers, flowers and more. This year, the blueberries and raspberries survived the winter and their fruit is plumping up. Two slicing tomatoes were transplanted, but the majority of the plants are annual flowers: salvia, amaranth, strawflower, dahlia, celosia, tulsi, lemon grass, marigold, and Sweet William. Some of the perennials include yarrow, violets, geranium, astilbe, and other semi-shade and shade lovers as there is a big umbrella of a maple on the west end. The pulling of weeds in front of the restaurant is happening now (after a good soaking rain) and then on to attacking the very front garden near the road. What should be planted there? I think sunflowers—what do you think?

No matter where you sow a seed, enjoy the journey; grow and nurture life. Just do it!

Next stop is the Cape Neddick garden at the Talpey Homestead. What does this garden grow for the season? Well, besides some destructive cutworms chopping on the baby beets there are three rows of potatoes including "Magic Molly" and "Dark Red Norland," sunflowers, pumpkins, winter squash, summer squash, beets, carrots, broccoli and a long row of cutting flowers. This fenced garden is 80 X 40 feet. The soil is fairly sandy and with all the wind and sun this garden can dry out quickly making carrot growing a bit challenging. The seeds will not germinate if it is too dry or the little seedlings will wither and die. Remember the trick in growing carrots? Continual moisture on the row or bed. I water daily (unless it rains) for nearly two weeks to let the carrot babies get a good start.

At home we are eating garlic scapes, Romaine lettuce, Swiss chard, parsley, radishes, edible pod peas, asparagus and scallions. The kale, onions, blueberries, raspberries, tomatoes and cutting and perennial flowers are all in various stages of growth. Having sunshine has helped the plants develop which now seem to be happy and healthy. The cherry tree is ladened with fruit—now to keep the birds from stealing our future bounty.

BE HAPPY

I found a place that touched my soul
The woods, the fields the meadows hold
The key to life and love and peace,
A key of gold–a soul feast!
So take your walk and stroll on down
The wooded path, before you drown
From negative chat and visual lie,
That rather, quite skews one by and by.
Let us reach out instead, to walk and grasp and feel this good earth
That rejuvenates us, giving rest and mirth!

The last garden is at the old Arrows restaurant, near Ogunquit. First Hill Gardens is now the Arrowheads Estate wedding and event venue. Some people said the gardens were "abandoned" or "neglected" for three to four seasons so you can imagine the weeds. I much rather say that the garden beds just were not planted and tended with disintegrating tarps, deer issues, etc. It is a beautiful setting and with care and time the garden beds will be much happier, less weedy and productive. Bees, birds and beneficial insects will abound.

Gardening in different locales sure is interesting. Each place has its own micro-climate, soil type, critter problem, insect infestations and specific weeds. Nearly all the seedlings going into all these gardens were started from seed and nurtured by me. I consider them to be my little babies and take great offense when the deer chomp their heads off. It is so rewarding to see the plants

take root and become prolific providers of food or even happiness for humans. The sunny, beautiful flowers conjure up a smile indeed. Happy Summer in the garden.

22
Dig 'Em Up

As people move closer to their food sources (farmers market, farm stand, CSA, growing their own) they are inevitably becoming educated in how certain vegetables are grown. For instance, take garlic.

More and more people now know about the curled, tender and mild flavored garlic scape or the flower stalk of hard neck Rocombole garlic.

The scapes are a hot item at the markets in May-June. The scapes are abundant as growers cut them off to encourage growth in the developing bulbs for larger garlic cloves at harvest time in July. There is a large number of ways to use them: pesto, dip, veggie stir fry, on the grill, etc. When young and tender, their flavor is mild. As they grow in diameter and length, they become sharper, more garlicky tasting, and the stems also toughen up.

We have used the straight, tougher scapes as skewers on the grill. The rigid scape lends a nice garlic flavor to the vegetables, scallops and shrimp we cooked.

If the scapes are not cut off the garlic plant, they grow toward the sky into long stems that eventually flower and develop into bulbils, which are tiny seedy bulbs that can also be planted. The bulbils usually take two to three years before maturing into a garlic bulb.

The tall elegant scapes look lovely growing in the garden, and I often use them in bouquets. Now this is when people really get stumped. Many people at the market have no clue what they are at this stage of growth and some people have no idea garlic grows deep in the ground.

At this time of the year I love to have a freshly dug garlic bulb with the stem and tall scape intact to use as a visual presentation to help customers put all the pieces together—sort of a Garlic 101 class.

In a nutshell, the life cycle of a garlic clove begins in October, when gardeners plant a single garlic clove previously harvested in July. After preparing the bed by adding compost and soil amendments the planted cloves are covered with leaf or straw mulch. The garlic clove winters in the soil, and then sprouts and grows above ground as one of the first signs of spring. The garlic plant grows a scape, which is then cut off in late spring in my garden. The garlic is harvested in July when the entire plant is dug up and dried for storage. The harvested July garlic will once again be planted in October before the ground freezes, continuing the cycle.

May we live, learn, sow, cultivate and reap abundantly – whether it be simply sowing garlic or whether it be sowing peace, gratitude and love. May your garlicky peace and love sprout every spring and grow tall and strong as the scape.

So how do you know when it's time to harvest? Look at the leaves that grow along the stem of the garlic plant. If about half of the leaves are dried and brown (from the bottom of the stem up), then it is about the time to harvest. It is also the time to harvest when the remaining scapes reach sky high and are developing their bulbils.

If you dig up the garlic too early, the cloves will be immature and it won't store quite as well. If you wait too long the bulbs start to separate, and they may sprout and not store so well either, so picking the right time to "dig em up" is something that is uniquely dealt with every summer.

So whether you are just learning about garlic or are especially savvy, enjoy every part of the garlic journey—it's quite a process! Good luck.

23
Wind

You may now know a bit about my gardening background. It started in the Hudson River Valley and at Camphill Village located west of the Berkshires and east of the Hudson. Then I gardened in the green, rolling hills of West Virginia. I have lived in York for thirty-seven years. Do you know what the first and most noticeable difference between locales was? Besides the lay of the land, ocean versus mountain, native vegetation and type of soil, a difference that literally struck me in my face when I moved here. It was the wind.

I used to garden in protected valleys between hills or mountains and wind was not thought of much, unless we had a good old-fashioned thunderstorm with a few leaves or small branches blown about and a tomato or two tipped over. When I moved near Nubble Lighthouse not only was it really chilly in the spring, but it was darn windy making it even colder! Wind not only can drop the temperature, but wind can also dry out the soil and can also structurally damage plants.

> **During windy and stormy times we may need to make a few adjustments and maybe we will learn a thing or two in the process. Take a deep breathe, take a step back, tie down the hatches. May the wind that we pour forth be good natured and respectful, never damaging. If needed, however, let the wind be filled with passion for justice, truth and respect for our earth. Let these winds blow strong and spread mightily.**

After a really heavy rain, thankfully the sun and wind is helpful in drying out the soil. It is great for flying kites, for filling a sail, knocking the bugs down and cooling us off. I do love the wind but not the cold, damp wind of late spring. All we want is warmth and to get our plants transplanted out into the garden. I guess all gardeners are faced with many lessons to learn—one being patience and respect (or is that humility?) during stormy times or windy events.

Oh yes, if you are new to southern Maine, we have had two mighty micro-bursts with really significant wind damage. The storm uprooted deciduous trees and many pines. We were all extremely lucky that no severe human injuries occurred. The plants in my garden were minimally damaged and I am happy to say the veggies survived the shock of wind and hail. Hopefully this summer and many more summers to come, will be free of severe weather like these microbursts. Please just give us a good old-fashioned thunderstorm instead. Thunder, lightening and some wind.

Here are some tips for new gardeners who would like to keep things upright: stake your plants, tie them up to a wooden, metal or bamboo stake or post or fence; construct a trellis or use a cage or whatever it takes to prevent wind damage. Fasten them well and reinforce the stakes. Growing tomatoes in a sturdy greenhouse is ideal. Besides nice and warm, you can control the amount of water on the plants and generally the wind is not an issue. Happy summer gardening.

24

Full Life and Full Gardens

It is amazing the amount of time that goes into gardening—the time it takes to grow vegetables, flowers, fruit, berries and herbs.

In addition to my garden at home, I am excited to be gardening in another plot in Cape Neddick at Faith Webster's homestead, also known as the Talpey Farm. Faith's perennial gardens, fields and forest will be written about in another essay—they are so very beautiful and unique. An exciting adventure this summer—as I am not a vendor at the York Farmer's Market—was a road trip to Virginia to visit the Spikenard Farm Honeybee Sanctuary in Floyd. Spikenard is quite an amazing place where humans learn so much from one another and from the bees. In the near future I will be putting thoughts to paper—you will get to experience Spikenard through my eyes.

It is an abundant time of the year for sure. Growing well this year: fennel, cucumbers, blueberries, garlic, asparagus, brussel sprouts, raspberries, kale, bush beans, summer and acorn squash, onions, swiss chard and flowers such as marigolds, zinnias, dahlias, sunflowers, strawflowers and statice.

Plants that were or are struggling in various ways are tomatoes, lettuce, eggplant, potatoes, celery and broccoli. The struggles with the plants vary between four-legged creatures, winged creatures and crawly creeping creatures, namely, tomato horn worms, a woodchuck, aphids, lace (or is that spotted?) wing drosophila, to name the main culprits.

The woodchuck decimated a row of broccoli in the Cape Neddick garden but the side shoots are growing so there will be some to eat. In the past I have caught groundhogs in Havahart traps, luring them in with broccoli (!) and camouflaging the top of the trap with comfrey and placing it right on the path the creature frequents. I wear gloves to leave no scent. The CN garden is fenced in but the wire was hanging low and the smarty pants woodchuck snuck in. The fence is now properly fixed blocking entry.

Take the time to study the small things in our gardens of life; see the parasitic wasp eggs on the back of the horn-worm, look at the spider web that caught the aphid, the pollen loaded bumblebee. Life is precious and fleeting. Preserving this delicate balance between insect, four-legged creatures, birds, beasts and humans may be our most important work on planet Earth.

The flies love fruit, so of course they are swarming on the raspberries (they will also land on blues and other berries). The trick with raspberries is to pick them DAILY and toss them in the freezer. Pick every ripe or near ripe berry. All over-ripe ones that usually have larva in them are tossed in the trash. Eat all the others now and the frozen raspberries in the winter. Keep the canes and ground beneath them clean, clean, clean with no fly debris. I learned these tricks from my neighbor Sharon, who learned it from her dad Everett.

Hornworms get picked off the plants—look for the scat and look up from there. They are evasive, especially if they crawl to another plant via a branch that is close by.

Aphids, aphids, aphids! Or are they white flies on the potatoes? Need to take the "looking glass" into the garden with an ID book. Definitely aphids on the brussels sprouts and the leaves of the potatoes were covered with flying insects that sucked the life out of the leaves. A cool, wet spring followed by dry spells and fluctuating temperatures apparently made for an insects' paradise. I hose off the bugs and various soapy insecticides can be used. Little spiders, lady beetles, wasps and bees are very happy and besides pollinating seem to be ingesting some non-beneficial insects. I like to let them do their thing in the garden. No soap on any of these beneficial guys and gals. Anyway, sap-sucking insects have struck the garden.

The cool, wet spring and early summer weather, plus the salt marsh mulch hay, set up a perfect storm for the slugs to multiply and devour many a head of lettuce. Don't mulch is my mantra for next year. Or put out more beer traps, or space things further apart—and I haven't even mentioned powdery mildew, or the birds or the chipmunks!

So, that is it in a nutshell. Eating well, weeding, harvesting, disease control, pest control, planting successively are all very time consuming activities.

25

Weeds—Not Always the Bane of Your Garden's Existence

Weeds. Are weeds a plant that you do not want growing in your field, flower or vegetable garden? Are they the bane or scourge of a gardener's existence? Do you call them your enemy and need to eradicate them? Why do farmers and gardeners not like weeds?

That is precisely what I did. I questioned the purpose of their existence in my gardens. I was one of the people who waged war on weeds, off and on, for many years. Crowding out of delicate or young vegetable seedlings was my main reason for pulling small weeds to make room for the growth of the adolescent plants. Freshly transplanted seedlings need room to grow and they don't want to be taken over by other plants like morning glory or crab-grass. The young transplant needs sun, water and all the nutrients available in the soil to uptake into the root system.

In the last few seasons, I have been looking at weeds in a new light. I have found that many of the "weeds" in my garden are medicinal and edible. Plantain (Plantago major) leaves are edible and contain Vitamin C along with some calcium and potassium and can be made into a poultice to help minor wound healing. It is a beautiful plant with seed spikes and a healthy root system. Purslane (Portulaca oleracea) is prolific and has a spreading, flat appearance on the ground. Purslane contains beta-carotene, Vitamin E and Omega 3 fatty acids. Nibbling on purslane may have health benefits. (Always correctly identify each and every plant or mushroom before ingesting any foraged find!)

What is growing in your garden? Do you have weeds that need pulling to make room for more growth or are some of your weeds beneficial and offer a healthy, symbiotic relationship in your garden of life?

Things I have learned from the weeds in my garden: some weeds help hold moisture in the soil and benefit the vegetable plants that are growing, such as sugar snap peas. This helps during our periods of no rain. Peas love it cool and the weeds help cool the pea vines as well. Weeds are opportunistic, adaptable, drought resistant or flood resistant. They make a nice path to walk on and the root systems break up hard-packed soil. I will always pull certain weeds, especially before they go to seed, but some I will leave, hopefully learning something new each and every growing season.

26

Rain Saved the Day—And the Plants!

This growing season has been a season of firsts. In particular, the driest May and June that I have ever experienced. We growers, farmers and gardeners generally have a statement that covers all the ups and downs of growing: "Well, there is always something!" And indeed, there always is; whether beast or bug or hail or wind—there is always something that must be dealt with.

In the Village of York, it got bone dry. For nearly seven weeks, we had about three rain showers that looked promising, but did not materialize. The thunderstorms went north and south of us. There was virtually no rain water in the rain gauge. Talk about disappointment.

The temperatures even hit 90 degrees and, with the wind, damaged the tips of the peas, stressed the plum tree, dried out the Lady's Mantle and generally turned lawns into deserts.

Out came the hoses, rain barrels, irrigation systems and watering cans. I have to say getting tangled in hoses, decapitating plants and lugging the heavy hoses is not my cup of tea. I have a meter to divert the water that goes into the garden from the water that goes into the septic system, lowering the town sewer fee a wee bit. That meter was whirring! I feel blessed to have water and the garden sure appreciated it, but there is nothing, absolutely nothing, like a good soaking rain.

THE CREEK

It is amazing we did not drown
with raging waters and debris abound!
The leaves, the twigs, the branches fell
and with it all there was the swell.
The swell and power of the water's course
was jagged, rough and full of force
Against our bodies, but not our minds,
we traversed the rapids over time.
The give and take, and push and pull
gave us pleasure, excitement, thrill!
Meandering down an unseen world of teeming
creekish rife,
We headed out to capture life!

A week ago we got just that—two inches fell over two days and it pretty much saved us. I loved not pulling out a hose to water the gardens. In the Cape Neddick garden, there is an artesian well and with hand watering most plants survived and many thrived.

That garden received 0.75 inches of rain about three weeks ago and then 1.25 inches last week.

The August weather we were having has now turned back into early June weather with cool temps and fog. I love a foggy day now and again, and I know we are in Maine, but the plants don't like being continually damp. Dampness inevitably equates to a fungus among us.

What would be perfect? A soaking rain, say one or two inches, one time per week. The potatoes, tomatoes, broccoli, beets, radishes and I would love it.

> **Plants send out tiny roots, bend their heads when stressed and patiently wait. Being flexible, resilient and creative can get us through these drought-like times, too.**

27

Surviving a Dry Spell

We started the growing season with a deficit. With little snowfall this winter and no abundant spring rains in April, we were and still are, in a dry spell. Three weeks ago we had a plant saving rain of two inches that put us a step ahead. Since then on two separate days it "showered" with 1/10 of an inch falling which basically hit the ground and evaporated (a rain gauge is very accurate). The wind, warm temperatures and sun have dried out the earth. One step forward and two steps back. The plants of course still appreciated every drop that fell during that soaking rain and the subsequent sprinkles thereafter. Generally speaking, plants like about 1 inch of rain per week, especially potatoes when they are forming their roots. And recently transplanted shrubs, vegetable seedlings and trees need lots of water perhaps every other day. So you wonder, how is anything growing without rain?

In Martha's Garden there are a few strategies that seem to be helping:

✿ Mulch, in this case, straw, placed around the base of the plants after a good soaking rain or hand watering helps prevent evaporation and keeps the roots damp. The tomatoes, beans, eggplants and peppers seem to be growing well with this mulch and minimal hand watering. It is also a great weed barrier preventing most weeds from germinating thus saving the gardener time and energy. The straw holds in moisture enabling the vegetable plants to flourish.

✿ When planting out seedlings such as tomato or broccoli plants, after you gently tamp down the soil around the plant, make a circular "trough" or indentation into the soil with your hand or hoe. This makes the soil directly around the plant lower than the rest of the soil. When it rains the water will collect within the circle and the water will more efficiently settle down into the roots.

Whether we have a deficit or an overabundance, let us be grateful for waking in the morning, treading on the dry or saturated earth and grateful for sitting down to a nutritious vegetable laden meal. Happy Summer!

✿ The peas are planted in hedges with numerous pea plants close to each other keeping the vines cool. I allow some "weeds" or volunteers like purslane and dill to grow in the hedge with the peas, as this appears to help hold in some water and also keeps the pea vine temps down. Peas love it cool and not hot such as it gets in the middle of the summer.

✿ I usually thin the raspberry canes, but this year they got ahead of me. At this time they are pretty happy because with more foliage it seems that there is more moisture due to less evaporation from wind and sun.

✿ I do water the plants with a garden hose. I actually love to use a hose if I have time—it is relaxing and satisfying to see the vegetables perk up with water (of course there is nothing like a soaking rain—you can nearly see the plants grow!). Certain nozzles with various settings may allow one to focus the water in a certain stream to be more efficient while using a garden hose. With mature plants I usually fill the water can and hand water just the roots of the plants to save water and to not get the foliage wet as I feel that a fungus might like the wet environment on the leaves and take up residence. Soaker hoses that get "planted" in with the row work well as the water is directed only on the roots—I will be setting up a soaker hose in the potato rows and for the onions. Potatoes that are deeply planted (often in small hills) need a good inch or more of water once per week to produce a nice sized root.

✿ Some plants have not received any extra watering such as the raspberries, mint, fruit trees and many other perennials such as yarrow or the peonies. All the baby seedlings are watered regularly. The blueberry bushes are also given a drink since their root systems are not exceptionally deep and dry out quickly. In dry spells it may be essential to water all your plants depending on how stressed they are. Look at the leaves, stems and fruits. Are the leaves wilted or the fruit looking dry? Dig into the earth. Hold the soil. Does it blow away like sand? You will be able to tell just by looking and feeling which plants need extra attention.

✿ Cooler nights and dew that has settled on the garden each morning has also been helpful to keep the plants alive.

28
Swiss Chard

The farmers markets are bustling this time of the year with greens, greens and more greens. And after a heavy rain the other day and a good dose of sunshine, Martha's Garden vegetables have started to explode into leaf. You can nearly see the plants growing or the flower blossoms opening to greet the day.

The root systems of the celery, kale, collards and lettuce are finally "taking root" and getting established, drinking up moisture and nutrients and allowing the upper structure to grow into an edible vegetable that is now quite identifiable. The young leaves are tender and nutritious, adding a nice color to any meal. Yes, any meal — even breakfast as some people may add chopped kale to their omelet, for example.

I am particularly fond of Swiss chard (Beta vulgaris, cicla group) since it is so pretty and sort of regal in its growth and upright stature in the garden. Swiss chard generally grows all season. As you cut stalks, other tiny stems grow into numerous mature stems. Chard provides you with a continuous harvest all summer long until a deep freeze. It is packed with vitamins C, A and K (K helps keep our bones strong in combination with calcium, boron, etc.) and has antioxidants to support our immune systems. It doesn't have a strong overwhelming taste and goes nicely in soups, frittatas, casseroles or as a single dish. It can be simmered, sautéed or braised. Here is a very easy recipe you can use for preparing Swiss chard:

> With summery sunny days approaching, may your hearts be happy and filled with light. Oh yes, and don't forget to eat your greens.

✿ Start gently sautéing two cloves of chopped garlic in three tablespoons extra virgin olive or avocado oil.

✿ Wash a large bunch of chard in water; shake the water off, dry a bit.

✿ Chop the stems and add them to the sautéing garlic carefully as not to have the oil splatter; let them get a bit tender and then add the chopped leafy part.

✿ Cover with a lid; stir often. If sticking to the pan, add some more oil or a little water to gently steam the leaves and stems; some people like it crunchy, others like it well done and tender.

✿ Add sea, pink or gray salt and pepper to taste.

✿ Serve piping hot as a side dish to your meal; it goes nicely with egg dishes, fish, chicken or any meat you may be serving.

✿ Enjoy the sunshine and warmer temperatures. Enjoy the abundance of vegetables that are being harvested. Soon there will be new potatoes, garlic scapes and beautiful lavender flowers.

29
From Weeds to Abundance

Let's discuss how a weedy and grassy area (a field or lawn) can be turned into a productive garden.

Over the years I have used a technique called soil solarization to turn grass or even a field into a tillable area. When I started solarizing, about 25 years ago, I didn't call it this fancy name. I used heavy ⅛-inch thick PVC lumber sheets that measured 10 x 4 feet and placed a couple on the ground in the spot where I wanted to plant vegetables or flowers. Usually I did this in the fall and left it in that spot all the way through the winter and removed it in the spring. So what happens? The weeds and grasses are smothered or heated up by the sun and die off. I am very good at killing grass and turning our lawn into a garden.

Over the last three summers I moved the technique to the Talpey Homestead's old veggie garden that had been left fallow

Whichever technique you use to cultivate your garden of life, may the outcome be peaceful and productive.

and converted back into a field. I spread thinner black heat-absorbing lumber tarps here, there and everywhere and "killed off" an area that measures 80 X 40 feet. I did not have a plow, couldn't fit a tractor through the gate, nor was I going to dig up this large area by hand. The black tarps absorb heat from the sun and heat whatever is beneath them. This includes weed seed, seedlings such as various grasses, plant pathogens including fungi and bacteria and some insects such as mites. This is the desired effect. The undesirable effect is that the worms high tail it out of the area and the good microorganisms are also killed along with the undesirables. Over time the worms will reappear and the soil will be teeming with microscopic organisms that will be beneficial to the plants. Compost and various soil amendments were added to each row this season and compost will be used yearly.

The technique is as follows: In the spring or fall, place a tarp or clear plastic (spring or summer the clear plastic works quickly!) in the desired area and weigh down with rocks, wood or large staple pins. Let the sun heat up the area—check under the tarp to see the progress. Some years the voles or moles helped kill off the weeds and grass by tunneling under the cover—this is about the only time the voles have been helpful. Next, after the area is heated up and looks like the weeds are dead, rake the debris out and then till it up or turn by hand. Remove any roots and plants that look viable.

If you don't want to use plastic, large pieces of cardboard may work to smother weeds. My father used old hay bales that were left outside for about a year. He broke off "slices" of the wet decomposing hay and laid them end to end. This technique seemed to work for him. And it works for me as well.

Solarize, rake, rake some more. Dig out stray weeds with a fork or shovel then till, plow or hand turn. Feed the soil with compost, cover crops, seaweed. Amend the soil if needed, plant and reap what you sow.

FALL

30
Cranberries—More American than Apple Pie

My assumption is that most of you reading this essay do not have this particular plant growing in your garden. I have a hunch, however, that you are very familiar with it in a culinary sense, since this fruit is more American than apple pie. It is a berry that complements pumpkin and turkey. You've got it—cranberry.

I have ten Howes American Cranberry or *Vaccinium macrocarpon* growing in a small raised bed. I bought the live plants from Fedco, the Maine seed, tree, tuber, and supply company. American cranberry plants are beautiful low-to-the-ground, creeping vines with tiny evergreen leaves that turn various shades of maroon and red in the fall. Bees pollinate the pretty little flowers; the honeybees and I love these ground covers.

Vaccinium macrocarpon likes acidic soil such as what our blueberries thrive in and are native to North America. Cranberries are found from Canada down to the higher elevations of North Carolina, related to bilberry, blueberries and huckleberries and the name is derived from what the European settlers called "craneberry" because the flower, stem and petals looked like a crane's head, neck and bill. Another name is "mossberry" and the North Europena variety *Vaccinium oxycoccus* is aptly named "fenberry", since it grows in a fen, also known as a marsh or bog. Ask me about my family name Fenn and the bog dwellers.) Bears eat the berries and some people call cranberries "bearberries".

The maple, birch, beech and oak have leaves still clinging fast, soon to be taken down by the gusty winds. The yellow, brown and red leaves will subsequently drop and cover the tiny red leaves of the cranberry making a carpet and collage of colors that will insulate and protect. Our observations are important to support the life of the plants, birds, and animals humans wildly need. I will keep my eyes open to the beauty and bountiful world that surrounds us.

American cranberries are shallow rooted and surprisingly can grow in dry soils, but prefer moister conditions. Raised beds can dry out very quickly, so I have had to water at certain times. Mulching with pine needles or leaves, helps keep in moisture and the dry winter winds out. The flooding of the fields of commercial growers is done annually for frost protection and to make harvesting the berries a whole lot easier. It is not necessary to do this in the home garden—just pick them by hand before a hard, killing frost. The first year I picked about ten berries, then the second year a small handful; the third year's "harvest" was a whopping two cups plus. Cranberries can be used fresh, frozen, dried, stored in the refrigerator, etc.

Indigenous people made pemmican with dry deer meat, fat and fenberries, used the berries as a dye and to treat wounds. They introduced cranberries to the Europeans, Abraham Lincoln declared a national Thanksgiving in 1863 and cranberries have adorned out tables for many decades. I am most familiar with cranberry sauce, breads, scones, juice, jellies, and stuffing. Health benefits include the following: Vitamin C, fiber, manganese and perhaps most importantly they have a phytochemical (flavonoid) proanthocyanadin, which allegedly prevents bacteria from adhering to the epithelial cell walls of the urinary tract preventing and healing urinary tract infections. The cranberry has small amounts of essential micronutrients and may have other antimicrobial properties as well.

My favorite formula for eating them: pop three berries in one's mouth and chew. What is yours?

31
Elderberry—Good for What Ails You

I grew up in the Hudson River Valley of New York State nestled between the Berkshires to the east and the river and Catskill Mountains to the west. The rolling hills, valleys, streams, farms and forests provided perfect conditions for plants, insects, birds and animals to thrive. As a child, crossing Stone Mill Road and heading down "the lane," one would see remnants of days gone by: stone foundations, very old weathered pear trees, previously cultivated grape vines and a decrepit turkey shed. Along the route, scattered hither and thither near the low-lying land by the creek, were tall shrubs ladened with white to cream-colored blossoms. These large flower heads produced tiny berries that my mother would make into wine and jelly. You would see these shrubs dotted along many country roads.

I learned that the clusters of blossoms I thought naturally

pretty and which looked like large Queen Anne's Lace, are called an umbrel. There are studies and anecdotal stories that indicate the blossom and berry, have beneficial immune properties. My siblings and I quickly learned what berries we could eat and which berries we could *not* eat. Elderberries were on the edible list after being simmered.

I have two really large elderberry bushes growing alongside my shed. I planted them to be sure I had a supply of berries to make syrup for the winter. The side benefit was "capturing" a piece of my parents' land and my childhood, bringing back the smell, feel and sensibility of things gone by.

The berries my mother picked were Sambucus, which is a genus of plants that produce flowers and is in the Adoxaceae family. Most likely, Mom's wild berries were not the European subspecies nigra but rather the native North American species called Sambucus canadensis. The flowers, which bloom in late June to July, are dried and made into tea to treat colds, sinus issues and bronchitis in part due to their anti-inflammatory and anti-microbial properties. The berries ripen in late August to September depending on Mother Natures' plan. Only ripe fruit is used as the un-ripened fruit contains toxic phytochemicals or cyanogenic glycosides, as do the leaves, seeds and stems. The berries are rich in calcium, iron, potassium, pro-Vitamin A and polyphenol antioxidants and can be cooked and made into jam or syrup. The cyanogenic toxins are found in smaller doses in mature fruit — they are destroyed by the heat in the cooking process. The Chippewa, Iroquois, and Cherokee indigenous people used the berries, leaves, inner bark, stems and flowers as food, medicinally for colds or fevers, poultices for minor skin problems, as an insect repellent, purple dye, spiles for sap collection and to wash their skin. Elderberries stimulate the immune system and may inhibit

a virus from entering and dividing inside human cells boosting respiratory health.

The two varieties of Sambucus Canadensis that are growing: "Adams" and "Johns". They love to grow in soil with a pH that is a bit acidic but will likely grow anywhere. If you have the space, go for it. They are nearly 10—12 feet high and about 5 feet wide shading everything near and far. So, beware, it literally grows overnight—Maine's Fedco Tree catalog says it is a "very large, vigorous, strong, productive bush." Indeed it is! Here's to your health and abundant growth!

32

Every Year is an Event-Filled year

What an incredible tomato year—hands down the best ever from my vantage point. There were dozens of fruit per plant and many plants are still ripening with a lot of green tomatoes. Green tomatoes are delicious fried or made into chutney.

Not only were the plants loaded with tomatoes, but the plants themselves looked beautiful (no fungi damage) despite a significant dry spell. Some of the prolific varieties grown this season: Rutgers (in honor of my Dad who graduated from Rutgers University with a degree in Poultry Husbandry), Jet Star, Amish Paste, Rose De Berne and Sun Gold. At the farmers' market tomato tasting, I came in a close second to the renowned grower Bill Connelly of Connelly's Organics. The only two hybrid tomatoes that I grew were enjoyed by the throngs who sampled the beautiful and sweet offerings from all the farmers' gardens. I am, year by year, switching most of my vegetables to open-pollinated varieties, but continue to hang on to my standby hybrids and old friends.

> Don't crush the parasitic wasp eggs piggy backing the tomato hornworm—this is Mother Earth's way to keep things in check. Let us look and listen carefully to nature; be thoughtful, respectful and honor the insects and animals that are so wise and wonderful.

Speaking of the "drought," it sure was dry and some days it got mighty hot! One Friday in August, while harvesting for the market, the thermometer registered 96 in the shade. I figured it was near 100+ in the sunny garden. That day a bathing suit, umbrella, water hose and cold showers came in handy. Oh, and lots of water to drink due to it being so bloody hot.

The plants found ways to soak up any moisture they could. It appeared that the tomatoes, which are fairly shallow-rooted, grew more shallow roots in all directions as occasionally (very occasionally) there would be a rain shower of about 1/10 of an inch. The sweet potatoes also sent out little hairy roots to grab whatever moisture was out there. I did have to water to keep various plants alive and since I am a small grower, was pretty much able to keep things going, unlike some farmers who had to choose between which crops to salvage and which to let burn up in the sun, wind and heat.

Another highlight of the season was the abundance of native pollinators such as bumblebees and wasps and our friends the honeybees. They were everywhere on the marjoram, Russian Sage, sun and garlic chive flowers. They seemed to be seeking water as well as pollen as they would be sipping a drink from the crook of a stem. This season I got stung numerous times, especially while picking raspberries—the yellow jackets and other insects were sucking the life out of the raspberry fruit gathering any water they could. The season was certainly challenging in more ways than one.

Other critters in the garden included wood chucks, deer, wild turkeys, chipmunks, domestic hens, domestic cats, voles, aphids and cabbage worms which I still am "embracing" or rather, dealing with. Another critter was the notorious tomato hornworm (actually tobacco hornworm or Manduca sexta) which can take down a full-grown tomato plant, fruit and all, if you don't find them and pick them off. The tomato hornworm is the caterpillar of the *Manduca quinquemaculata* or the hawk moth. Both are beautifully patterned and I wish not so destructive to the Solanaceae family. The absolute highlight (only a gardener would say this) was the finding of the Braconid wasp cocoons all over two tomato hornworms! The adult female parasitic wasp lays eggs just under the hornworms' skin and eventually wasps emerge killing the near four-inch hornworms. The wasps offer not only a natural predatory response to the destructive hornworms, but they also pollinate our fruits and vegetables. I consider this to be a win-win or good gardening situation.

So, that nearly wraps up the season. I nearly forgot—I was a vendor at the Common Ground Fair this year—I will have to tell you about the fair when I see you.

33

Frost is Coming

It is that time of the year when gardeners are out straight, wisely harvesting before a frost settles on the crops. Here in the Village of York, the date for a first frost is usually around mid-October but head a couple miles west, away from the ocean, and the frost will hit vegetables in September. Some crops such as kale and Brussel sprouts will actually improve in flavor and won't be bothered much until it gets really cold. At times, kale will survive or "winter over" and flourish for a time in the next gardening season. Some folks at the farmer's market mentioned they have been munching away on their homegrown kale that survived the winter. Tomatoes and other warm weather crops cannot tolerate cold and will be destroyed by a frost so picking them in advance of the frost is a very smart move indeed.

What vegetables are being harvested this fall? Here is a short list: Potatoes, onions, tomatoes, celery, peppers, sweet potatoes, broccoli, and eggplants. You are probably aware of the traditional ways of preserving or "putting food up or putting food by" such as freezing or canning. I would like to take a moment to talk about dehydrating. Dehydrating veggies and fruits removes the moisture by using a low heat source which preserves the vitamins and limits the growth of microorganisms. Dehydrating is another way to preserve food for the long winter and a great way to put up food from a garden that is overflowing with produce.

We have an electric Excalibur Food Dehydrator (a plastic and metal box with racks that electrically heats up and circulates air with a fan) and a booklet with instructions on how to prepare and dehydrate various fruits and vegetables. Some people simply use their baking oven, set at a very low temperature which can work very well. My experience with the commercial dryer started about seven years ago, so this is a relatively new process. I find cutting the veggies and laying them on trays a relaxing task. Be sure to use the lowest setting possible to take the moisture out—experimenting with the drying time by increasing the temperature a few degrees may cut down on the length of time it takes to dehydrate a particular vegetable or fruit. Cherry tomatoes and sweet peppers have been my main focus, but I have also tried celery, herbs, blueberries and kale chips.

The first step is to harvest. I pick about a dozen slender Jimmy Nardello sweet peppers that are very red and ripe. Next step: wash them well and pat dry. Slice them about 1/8 in. thick or so and place them on the trays. This is a great pepper to dehydrate as it is long and slender with a thin wall. This variety slices into workable "rings" that lay nice and flat on the racks; the rings look pretty, smell great and dry well. On the top of the dehydrator is a chart that tells you the temperature for drying

THE KEEPER OF THE WOODS

I live on the edge of the woods, but my heart always
remains smack dab in the middle.
I sleep within wooden walls during the dark hours.
During the light of day my feet carry me on
well trodden paths,
rays of sunshine bright in the clearing, warming skin,
sinew and bones.
Walking deeper with dappled light now—oranges
and yellows blinding my vision;
deeply receptive to the touch of the leaves from the
still shedding maple.
Open to the wind at my back, the sound of a distant
owl, caw of a crow.
Off the path I see coy wolf scat knowing the closeness to the den.
The coyotes know me now from a pact made long ago.
The deeper wood is denser, darker as November has settled in.
I can see some distance into the far reaches of the forest
from time to time.
Tall erect trunks remind my curved spine to stand taller,
to reach skyward.
The underbrush, litter and detritus make it hard to
stay balanced.
Concentrate on footing.
There we are.
A cairn, a testament to a life once lived well.
Buried here is where half my heart lies with ashes.

herbs, a particular fruit, etc. Just an easy twist of the knob starts the dryer. I always start low to preserve the nutritional qualities inherent in the produce and check frequently to see how things are progressing. There are other ways to dry food using solar energy—think sun-dried tomatoes. Sun drying may be a project in the not-too-distant future.

When the peppers are completely dry—look closely—you will feel very dry, shriveled rings that appear desiccated– let them cool down and immediately place in glass jars. Use them any way you wish: on homemade pizza, in soups, stews or in tomato sauce. Enjoy your bountiful harvest now and in the winter as you reap your rewards. The heady bouquet of a jar of dehydrated Jimmy N. in the middle of the winter is really something—an intoxicating whiff of summer during the dark days.

34
Garlic and Shallots—Get Planting Before the Ground Freezes

It is that time of year when the garlic and shallots need to be planted if a farmer, home gardener or market grower wants a crop next summer. This autumn has been exceptionally mild with no frost in my garden as of October 29. Perhaps the temperature this week will dip down low enough to chill all the abundant vegetables and freeze the flowers that are quite like energizer bunnies—they just keep on going! The warm temps, on the other hand, have made it delightful to plant the garlic and shallots roots without freezing the fingers.

The following is a tutorial on how to plant shallots and/or garlic.

✿ Prepare the soil. You can add compost and soil amendments now. I usually add the compost and amendments in each hole I dig or just add everything now at the time of tilling. Either till or hand turn the soil. I like to turn by hand, so the worms aren't disturbed. Rake out any rocks, roots, and weeds and discard or compost them (meaning weeds, not rocks).

A little work and preparation now could make a world of difference later.

✿ I use my own garlic that was harvested this season in July. I count out how many garlic and shallot bulbs I want to keep for the winter, then how many I need or want to replant for next year. Some varieties have four cloves and others have more, so I count each individual clove and separate the cloves from the bulbs. I plant hard neck varieties such as Music, German White and Russian Red; I have been experimenting with a soft neck variety but so far, the flavor is just not as delicious or sweet as the fresh hard necks that I grow. The French Gray (or is it grey?) shallots are easy to separate.

✿ I dig and screen my own compost or use compost that is purchased. I place the compost in buckets, soak the cloves in some water for 5 minutes or so (unless it is going to rain really hard), gather my hand tools, knee pad and if you want to add soil amendments (greensand, bone char) they can be added now or prepare to place in each hole that is dug. I keep the bucket of compost, mixed amendment bucket and container with the garlic or shallots right next to me as I plant and slide them down the side of the bed. I usually have an empty bucket to place rocks in. It is a back and forth, side to side motion and a lot of garlic can be planted in a pretty short time.

✿ Some people dig furrows and place each individual clove in the long trench and then cover the cloves with dirt. I like to prepare a bed and plant about four to six garlic cloves across the rectangular bed and then move backward adding short row after short row. I dig four to six holes with either my Korean tool called a Ho-Mi ("little ground spear") or a clawed hand cultivator. The holes are about six inches apart. I throw in one or two handfuls of compost and amendments in each hole and really fluff up the soil with my hand tool, place one clove root side down and pointed side up and cover with about four inches or more of soil so it is nicely mounded over the garlic or shallot. I pat the soil so it is firmly covered and think about how beautiful they will look as they grow out of the earth next spring. If you plant hundreds of cloves of garlic and dig each hole—this might be a bit much for your dominant hand and wrist. Preparing the bed by tilling in the compost and amendments might be the easier way, as you can just pop in the cloves and call it a day.

✿ You are not finished yet. Mulching is a must here in Maine. To protect the garlic or shallot cloves from severe cold that may damage the roots, a cover of straw or chopped up leaves about 4 to 6 inches or so will provide a decent cover. Be sure you don't mulch with regular leaves as it will be difficult for the shoots to push through the matted, large and wet leaves when the warmer temps arrive. I use mowed or chopped up pieces of maple leaves so the garlic can push through more readily. When Spring is here and the shoots are coming up, I will sometimes uncover them a tad just by taking my fingers and "raking" the chopped-up leaves from around the new garlic plant. Enjoy the process—it amazes me every season.

35

Garlic—Don't You Just Love It?

So, you say you don't like kale? Don't despair since the gardens are loaded with vegetables at this time of the year: tomatoes, tomatillos, leeks, turnips, chard, peppers, radishes, lettuce, spinach, arugula . . . you get the idea—many plants to showcase each week and one you may find delectable.

I have chosen one of the oldest cultivated plants in the world, garlic, to have a chat about. It is planted now in preparation for next year's harvesting, so it is heavy on a gardeners' mind. With this gorgeous warm weather, frost may not be on your mind, but the inevitable will happen, and the garlic better be in the ground before the ground freezes solid. A bonus to planting the garlic when there is some warmth in the air—your fingers don't freeze!

Garlic is also known as *Allium sativum*—the "al" of allium from the Celtic "al" meaning "burning." This allium genus' close relatives are onions, leeks, chives and shallots; garlic is in the lily family Sativum meaning "harvest or cultivate." Garlic has a long, rich and diverse history dating back about 7,000 years with references made linking garlic to the Egyptians, Babylonians, Phoenicians, Romans and Vikings. For instance, the workers who built the pyramids ate radishes, onions and garlic (as did soldiers and sailors and others) for strength and courage. Garlic has been known as a cosmic symbol, has been used by ancient Egyptian and Israelites, and mentioned in an ancient Greek play. Hippocrates, Pliny the Elder and others were really excited about garlic.

Whatever seed you plant, deep or shallow, may it grow and flourish.

There are several references that indicate garlic originated in western or central Asia, possibly in the Kirgiz desert region of Siberia, then brought to Asia Minor and on to Egypt by nomadic people, then through India via the trade routes to Eastern Asia and to Europe.

So, what is all this fuss about anyway? It appears that in history (and currently) people either liked or hated garlic; garlic was good, or it was evil. Garlic was used medicinally to treat numerous ailments, including digestive disorders, parasites, respiratory infections, low energy, etc. Pliny the Elder, a Roman naturalist, was a huge advocate of remedies incorporating garlic as the main ingredient. Garlic has antibiotic, anti-viral, anti-fungal and antiseptic properties due in part to the sulphur containing allicin, which also gives it that stinky odor.

Garlic contains phosphorus, selenium, vitamin C, manganese, vitamin B6, potassium and zinc (think health-producing, anti-inflammatory and antioxidant properties!). The head of garlic or bulb is made up generally of four or more cloves encased in a paper-like covering, which can be used for culinary purposes, medicinally or as a natural insecticide in the garden. Additional

health benefits may include improvement in cardiovascular health, healing cold sores, lowering of blood pressure, preventing clots, soothing psoriasis, fighting viral infections, and garlic may be a cancer preventative. The components of garlic such as allicin and alliin are among the allyl polysulfides that give garlic its many beneficial properties. I never knew that some people are "allergic" to garlic causing diarrhea and intestinal pain. Thankfully I am on good terms with the root.

My connection with garlic is through a grower's eyes and a garlic lover's taste buds. Allium sativum is one of the very first plants to truly show us that, indeed, spring is on its way. I so love to see the first three green leaves of the plant "springing" through the soil. I love to watch the plants grow taller, stronger and to notice the first signs of the scapes that are generally snipped off to encourage bulb growth. Garlic scapes have become a hot item at the farmers markets and in our kitchens. When curled, young and tender they are great grilled, in a stir fry or made into a pesto. If

left on the plants they unfurl into tall strong stems with the flower head or umbrel, which develop into bulbils or very tiny garlic seeds that can be planted. I plant the single cloves in October which develop into heads by the following July. There are soft and hard-neck varieties, large and small varieties, varying colors, heat and spiciness. Garlic gardeners must experiment to find what works for them. I love to taste the fresh-harvested garlic that is sweet and juicy. Over time the garlic becomes hotter and can even be bitter when raw or sautéed.

I love the anecdotal input from people about garlic. I mostly hear about its anti-viral effects: people chew it, put it in soups, combine it with local honey, chug it down. With cold and flu season upon us, be sure to eat your garlic!

Besides chewing a raw clove (beware of the heat!) this is how I use garlic to ward off the flu and colds viruses and keep my immune system strong:

✿ Make a chicken stock with chicken bones.

✿ In a big pot, cover the bones with filtered, well or spring water, I add about 2 tsps. apple cider vinegar; be sure you have plenty of water in the pot.

✿ Add two or three bay leaves, two or more cloves of garlic, one good-sized onion, throw in a shallot or two, garlic scapes, add whatever herbs are in your garden or fridge, such as thyme, marjoram or rosemary.

✿ Add two celery leafy tops and stalks and a carrot cut in half.

✿ Add some sea salt or pink Himalayan salt, pepper if you wish.

✿ Simmer at least four hours (often for 8 hours in this house) then strain threw fine strainer, pick off meat and throw chicken meat back in the broth, discard or compost the rest.

✿ Add to the broth/stock freshly cut up celery, carrots, maybe turnips or other vegetables you prefer, a few sprigs of thyme and other herbs, simmer a bit.

✿ Then throw in a handsome handful of parsley and please note: add fresh garlic — be sure to break the cell walls down by putting through a press or kind of pulverizing the garlic on your cutting board as this activates the cells to produce allicin which gives garlic its aromatic smell.

✿ I might add some small pieces of fresh greens—what else but kale!

✿ Season with salt and pepper, depending on your taste buds, and enjoy the warming qualities of chicken soup. Eat it soon after adding the garlic to get the benefits of the nearly raw root.

Read about garlic, experiment with your recipes. If you don't care for it, don't despair, there will be another vegetable that will likely float your boat.

> Just as the sun rises in the morning, as the garlic winters over in the frozen earth and the sun sets tonight in the west —the North winds will surely blow. Sip a garlicky soup that warms toes and soul on some future cold winter night.

36

Happy Dahlia Digging Day

Years of crossing *D. pinnata* and *D. juarezi* has brought to the masses blossoms galore! The D. is for Dahlia which is related to our well-known zinnias and sunflowers—also the national flower of Mexico and the plant was used by the Aztec's as a water pipe. Originally a source of food, they were discovered in Mexico and crossbred by numerous people in places such as Europe. We now have hybrid flowers that range in size from about 2 to 12 inches. Some may stand as tall as 6 to 8 feet or as short as a foot.

These tuberous roots produce some mighty sturdy stems which takes a machete to cut them—well, at least a knife or sturdy clippers. The uprightness of the stems and beautiful blossoms represent dignity and stability. They have no scent that I have been able to detect. I visited the Topsfield Fair this year and there were hundreds of single stems in the flower show. It was very impressive and has given me ideas for what to grow next year. They make great cut flowers that hold up for at least three days or longer, if the ambient temperature is cool (such as in air conditioning or walk in cooler). Colors range from white, pink and purples to orange, yellow and salmon. There are solid, bi-color, double, "dinner plates," cactus, semi-cactus and decorative blossoms to choose from. Dahlias bloom from the middle of the summer right up to the first frost and add spectacular color to an autumn garden.

Take a look at the upright Dahlia and be reminded about dignity, uprightness and stability, which humans truly desire. Happy Dahlia Digging Day!

The thing to remember about Dahlias and New England is that the tubers need to be dug up before a really hard frost and wintered in a place where they won't get too cold nor where the mice might find them. I trim the stems off the tubers, leaving 1.5 feet, so I can get a grasp on the plant and lever the roots out of the ground with a fork or shovel. I dust off some soil, set them in the sun to dry for a couple of hours and knock some more dirt off the root cluster. Then I place them in the basement in large garden tubs in semi darkness at about 45 degrees F. Next spring, after the last chance of frost (usually in late May), the roots get divided, then planted about 3 to 5 inches deep with lots of compost mixed in. You may lay the tubers flat with the eyes up. I sometimes have them more upright; cover them with soil and give them a pat and a good soaking unless Mother Nature does this for you. They love sun but will grow in semi-shade with only 3 hours of sunshine.

So get those Dahlias out of the ground and protected until the next growing season. Now is the time.

37

It's a Beet, It's a turnip, . . . No, It's a Radish

If you have visited any Farmers Market you most likely have been introduced to a vegetable called a winter storage radish. This is exactly where I met 'Green Meat,' 'Watermelon,' and 'Misano Rose'—at Garens Greens at Riverside at the Portsmouth, New Hampshire market. Garen is a gardener who raised vegetables at Riverside Farm in North Berwick and now he grows them at Schoodic Hollow Farm in Franklin, ME. They are ubiquitous in CSA winter shares and in the fall and winter markets.

When you first take a look at these roots you may think it is a beet or turnip. The radish roots can be medium to large and round with various shakes of pink or rose. Some are long and cylindrical like 'Green Meat' (think Daikon and yes, it is green and white) and yet another variety I have grown is called "Black Storage." This is hefty and round with pure white flesh and a beautiful black exterior with a large dose of spiciness. I love the descriptions of the winter radishes in the Fedco Seed catalog using words such as "fine tasting, good looking, green apple flavor, plenty of spiciness, sweet vegetable undertone, small daikon," making it hard not to buy every single darn radish seed packet. They certainly have a special way with words! When I bite into a raw black radish my taste palette experiences quite a kick with spice—like flavors. When peeled, shredded and mixed with shredded carrots and ginger, sesame oil and chopped onion, the hot tang is tamed. Add any dressing you like making this a side dish or salad to accompany a main meal. Experiment with adding honey or vinegar and you may find that you really like the texture and flavor.

The hard freeze has hit the garden and what was is no more. Autumn is carrying us close to the cold winds of winter; the geese are migrating south. May our bellies and hearts be warmed with a spice-filled bite of storage radish slaw during the dark days of Winter.

Winter radishes are easy to grow, (You may need to cover the seedlnigs with a floating row cover to prevent flea beetles from decimating them.) store well in a refrigerator or root cellar and offer a freshness that is sublime in the middle of the cold season. July planting may mean a fall harvest. After dusting or washing them off and trimming the tops, place in the bottom drawer of your fridge or place in wet sand in your root cellar.

38

Plant Now for Next Year

Summer moved quickly—too quickly for my liking. The cool off at the end of July through August, then some nights in the thirties in September, really set things in motion for winter to arrive. Frost hit the gardens west of here about one week early in September, yet there have been lovely warm days at times easing our way into autumn with subtle offerings then vibrant colors, rustling leaves, for leaf peepers or gardeners to admire.

Now the oaks and birches are sharing their earthy hues—I have to admit I do love the fall and the slowing down of all things "garden." Clean up and more harvesting is on the "to do" list for sure, but the main focus now is to get the rest of the shallots and garlic planted so there will be a bountiful harvest next year.

Let's get started! Pick a sunny spot and clean up the area of your garden where you want to plant the garlic and shallots.

Dig up the weeds and get the roots entirely out of the ground so you have less to weed next year. Rake off all the debris and toss the weeds in your compost pile or have a separate pile for them. I have a lot of rocks, so I set them aside in small piles or sometimes just don't sweat it and leave them. Decide what soil amendment you wish to use—Fedco seed catalog has a "growers supply" section that you can peruse to study the various powders and fertilizers that help build a healthy soil (check on-line for other sites). Doing a soil test through the Cooperative Extension is a great idea to really know what might be lacking in your soil, what the pH of the soil is and what is needed in the soil for the plants to thrive.

The humble beginnings with a simple clove of garlic or shallot, placed in the ground, wintering through the cold and dark, to emerge into a thing of beauty and culinary delectability. Now this is something to ponder.

Organic gardeners and others use crop rotation, cover cropping and the addition of soil amendments to improve the vitality of the plants, decrease diseases, improve soil structure and increase the numbers of beneficial organisms living in the soil. The rock powders could, at times, supply a fairly quick fix if your soil is lacking a specific nutrient. There is Azomite, Boron, Greensand, Lime, Menafee Humates to name a few.

Please don't forget about your compost as this may be your best bet for growing a decent garden. Now dump the compost on the planting area (a good four inches or more) along with the necessary amendments and turn them into the soil or till them in. Most years I have dug the planting hole with the hand cultivator and have thrown compost and amendments into the hole and then planted the garlic clove. I usually plant the cloves about six inches apart or roughly the length of my hand "digger." I separate all my garlic bulbs or shallots into individual bulbs or cloves (saved from July's harvest) and go to town digging down into the earth about 4-6 inches. Add the compost and loosen the soil

then place one clove with the root side down and the stem side up into the hole. Cover with the loose soil and pat down. If you plant about six garlics across, you can end up with a nice rectangular garlic bed. You can run a string along the side of the bed to keep you on track or place a wooden board next to the bed to keep you from making a really crooked bed.

After the garlic or shallots are planted, I cover the entire bed with about four inches or more of shredded leaves ((maple), salt marsh hay or straw. This helps keep the severe cold from injuring the garlic and helps control the weeds in the spring. Whole leaves mat too much, and the garlic will have difficulty growing through them.

Look up on-line, in a seed catalog that sells garlic or in a good book for more details on planting, storing, etc. By the way, no frost has settled in my in-town garden as of this writing. I never, ever remember not having a frost by the middle of October—here in Maine or in upstate New York or in the rolling hills of West Virginia. I will let you know our frost date the next time around.

4
3
2
1

39

Maine Sure Was Dry Last Season

These are challenging times for sure. Gardening in Maine this season was especially so, as we had severe drought conditions. For nearly seven weeks in May and June, we went without measureable rain. Thankfully we received 2 inches in June that saved the gardens.

After June we did not have anything substantial, just a shower now and then (we did receive rain toward the end of the season) that evaporated off the surface of the gardens. The season's 90 degree temps, sun and wind dried out the gardens. The soil was like dust, blew in one's face and nostrils, and then floated away. With all the dust flying about, a face mask sure came in handy this dry season.

Lugging hoses around the gardens was a standard practice, week after week. Without town water or the artesian well water, the gardens would have completely fried. Some plants just did not make it—some squash plants, grasses, section of lawn, tips of edible peas and even some perennials shriveled and turned brown. The vegetables and cut flowers came out on top of the list as the plants that would receive water from "the hose." It took many hours some days to simply water one garden.

Water your roots, tend to the garden and enjoy every moment of this precious life!

Next year, the main hose will come down a path in the middle of the long garden rows and will be connected to a "splitter" or "Y" to which several hoses can be added and travel down the half rows. No more lugging really long hoses, down really long rows and destroying the plants on the ends of each row. Some sprinkler hoses will be neatly laid out with the potatoes or other crops that need at least one inch of water per week to grow well and size up. Hopefully I will have a custom-made table (Steve take note) to house an old sink for hosing off root vegetables. The water will flow into a 5-gallon bucket, and will be used to re-water the vegetables. Every drop is precious and conserving well water during a drought makes a lot of sense.

The dahlias and most other flowers did very well. Never have I watered flowers as much as I did this summer. In many of my photos, you can see the vibrant colors and various sizes and textures. It was a splendid flower-growing season. I hope your gardens were filled with vibrant color. The dahlia tubers will be pulled tomorrow and stored until next spring. Another season will be ending.

With the deep freeze a few days ago, nearly every flower blossom was hit. Just like that. It came late, but nevertheless it finally arrived with a bang.

40

Sow a Cover Crop

I was hoping for warm autumn temps to get the pumpkins and winter squash ripened up, and that is just what has happened. The squash and pumpkins were direct seeded late this year (July) but it all seemed to work out well. It remains an extremely busy time of the year with farmers harvesting their crops before the frost settles on the vine, planting cover crops, garlic and shallots. If you are lucky enough to have a greenhouse, then you will be extending the season into or through the winter months. Crops still prolific in Martha's Garden are: cool weather plants such as kale, chard, spinach, beets, arugula, leeks, shallots, lettuce, cilantro, brussels sprouts and tomatillos, tomatoes and celery. I harvested a bumper crop of gorgeous onions, garlic, acorn, spaghetti and butternut squash, red and French Grey shallots, four varieties of potatoes. The freezer is packed with wild Maine blueberries, cranberries, raspberries, and tomatoes. Our bellies will be well fed this winter. Adding to the larder will be the brussels sprouts, herbs, and anything else we can harvest before heavy frosts settle in the garden.

> **Nurturing the earth and enhancing this micro-friendly soil will provide a sound, healthy and happy environment—may it be "sow" in your garden of life as well as mine.**

Another successful crop this year is something I am very proud of, of all things, a cover crop. Yes, a cover crop specifically called Everleaf Oats. This oat can also be used as forage or food in the form of hay for animals, as a feed grain after it reaches its five feet height or as a cover crop also called a green manure. In the Fedco catalog they say, "These green manures take up and store nutrients to be used by subsequent crops, suppress weeds, host beneficial insects, improve the structure and arability of the soil, and can even break up clay and hardpan." This is quite the list of beneficial properties. The more common cover crops that you may have heard of are peas, buckwheat, rye, or wheat. I decided on the oats; so far, I am glad I did. If it rains or showers the seed has great germination. If there is a dry spell, then you may need to water the seeds for a couple of days to get them to sprout. I noticed the dew was helpful also. The leaves are lush and plentiful, look lovely and will provide some biomass. The cold will kill the plants, then in the spring the earth will be turned, and a crop planted in that spot. A goal is to build up the soil with microorganisms by feeding the soil with green manures, ultimately producing healthy plants that have nutritious qualities. I will let you know how the soil is improving over the years.

I have planted cover crops in the past but did not have much success with germination. In other words, it was basically a complete failure. I know why that was happening—the neighbors chickens used to eat all the seeds! No chickens in the garden this year means great germination.

41
Birds Love the Hawthorn Berries

I have been drinking Crataegus berry and hibiscus flower tea for several years. Turns out the berries may be high in antioxidants making it a good fruit to protect the heart and the immune system. I read that besides the berries, the young tender leaves and even the flowers are edible (salads or teas) and may also be important for a healthy heart.

The active, inherent compounds in hawthorn berries that may help blood flow to the heart and help the general functioning of the heart are flavonoids such as quercetin, rutin, and crataegolic acid, which is a terpene. There have been studies and reviews indicating that there are indeed positive results from ingesting these phyochemicals (always consult with your health care provider prior to ingesting any new herb, fruit or plant as it may be contraindicated or deleterious with certain meds or other herbs;

also correctly ID your plant when foraging.) The berries are used in traditional Chinese medicine and the Blackfoot, Lakota and Ojibwa, amongst other people, ate haws for food.

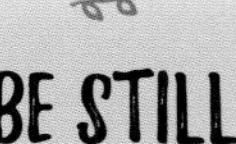

BE STILL

Be still.
Listen to the whispering wind, creaking
floorboards, crashing waves.
All around us the Spirit lives and breathes,
calling, beckoning.
The Spirit beckons us to act, to do, to be, to love.
Love surrounds us, love envelopes us.
Deeply inhale the seasons' offerings;
exhale into the world all that the earth needs.
Be still.

The genus Crataegus, from the Greek kratos for "strength" and akis for "sharp", is known as hawthorn, whitethorn or haw berry. This tree or shrub which is part of the the Rosaceae family of plants is naturally found in northern Europe, Asia and North America. "Haw" means "hedge" and more recently applies to the fruit. Here in New England we have about 45 hawthorn species but this is apparently debatable. A commonly known species is Crataegus chrysocarpa or fire berry hawthorn.

Hawthorn berries provide birds with winter food and the seeds are dispersed by the birds in other locales. Best known is the jelly or wine that can be made from the haws. The tree I harvested from was about 12 feet high with the corymb (dangling berries) pretty easy to pick off the lower branches. These trees

have long thorns that were used to make an awl to sew with, while fishhooks and bows can be made from the woody parts of the tree. The tree is pretty with white blossoms in May and dangling red berries provide beauty to the eye and soul. A pretty tree or shrub for your yard that the birds will love—just watch out for the thorns.

The second picking of berries is in the dehydrator and the first dry batch is sitting pretty in a quart jar. Winter is coming, so getting in the harvest from garden, field or woods is of the essence, before Ole' Winter visits us.

42

You Can't Beat What Beets Can Do for You

This vegetable is pretty darn fresh having sat in the bottom drawer of the refrigerator for the last two months. It is full of Vitamin A, B6, and C, fiver folate, magnesium, potassium, silica, phosphorus and iron. Wow. This mystery vegetable may be helpful in lowering blood pressure, fighting inflammation, helping digestion, increasing cognition, preventing constipation; is used as a food coloring and for sugar production. Wow again. What vegetable are we talking about here? *Ahhh!* The mystery vegetable is beetroot or taproot of Beta vulgaris, better known as red or golden beet.

Beet roots are loaded with phytonutrients, called betalains, and have plenty of antioxidants thus making them anti-inflammation helpers and just plain good for us. Some common cultivars or varieties are Detroit Dark Red, Chiogga, Early Wonder, Bull's

Blood, Golden Grex and Lutz Green Leaf. The red and green leafy "greens" are nutritious when sautéed or steamed as well as the root. The tiny seedlings can be thinned, and stems and root cooked until tender. Harvesting small beets helps the plants that are left, to grow into larger roots for later in the season. The early, small beets are very flavorful, not bitter and they are tender. Boil with the skins on, steam or roasted in the oven. Beets can be eaten raw as well. They can be pickled or made into a soup called borscht.

May we learn from those before us and learn to understand and know the inherent qualities of plant and animal. May we look at our fellow humans and still see our collective inherent qualities and may these positive qualities prevail.

Here's one way to cook beets:

1. Harvest six medium-sized beets from your garden, root cellar, through your CSA, store or farmer's market.
2. Cut off the stems leaving about one inch. This way they won't bleed so much. Save the beet greens in your refrigerator; cook them at another time just as you might spinach.
3. Scrub the beets with a stiff brush, rinse and place in a pot with two inches of water to cover. Bring to a boil and reduce the heat to a simmer. Simmer until al dente or fork tender. The time will depend on variety and size of the root—the smaller the faster they will cook.
4. Let them cool down a bit; rinse them under cold water and slip off the "jackets" and compost the skins.
5. Slice or cut into pieces, add butter, salt and pepper. Eat right away. Instead of butter you can sprinkle the roots with vinegar or a favorite dressing; serve hot or cold.

If you like raw vegetables, you might like a grated raw beet salad:

1. Scrub, wash and peel a beet.

2. Grate this one large beet into a bowl.
3. Grate 2 to 3 carrots in with the beet.
4. Add any homemade or store-bought salad dressing or mix sesame oil or olive oil with vinegar, salt, and pepper. You can add a handful of raisins, cashews, or parsley. Mix well.
5. Chill for a few hours. The fresh, earthy taste is refreshing, especially on a hot summer day.

WINTER

43

Dig into Homemade Soup

Wow, it sure gets chilly in New England after the year turns. With temperatures dipping near zero what possible time is this? *Soup Time* of course! Soup warms you when making it, while it steams up your house and especially when you sip it piping hot! The following are a couple of soup recipes that you might just like to dig into.

I love to make a squash soup since it is fairly easy and tastes delicious. Cucurbita moschata is generally my choice. You will know this squash by its more familiar name "butternut". Nearly any squash or even pumpkin can be substituted; acorn, buttercup, New England pie are great to try. These keepers store well in winter and are available at Farmer's Markets, winter CSA's or in grocery stores. For those people who may have severe arthritis or who are unable to cut the behemoth monsters, you can usually find them already cut for you. This makes the whole process much easier.

Here we go! Gather all your ingredients, cutting board, sharp knife, and a stainless steel pot or other pot that is non-aluminum.

Just a quick note—I usually don't follow recipes. I do change things in mid stream experimenting with spices and herbs—a pinch of this, a pinch of that—the "kitchen clog" that I like to dance. I'll try my best with measurements that you can understand.

✿ Start by sautéing one large chopped onion and two large smashed garlic cloves in about 3 Tbsp. of olive or avocado oil or fat of your choice.

✿ Add to the onion mixture: 2–3Tbs. cumin, ¼ tsp. grated nutmeg, ½—2 tsp. sea, Celtic or pink Himalayan salt, several good twists of the pepper grinder, 1 tsp. ground cardamom (mortar and pestle work well here), ¼ tsp. cayenne pepper or a smaller pinch, 1—2 bay leaves. If you love spices you can increase these amounts if you desire. Careful with the cayenne, as it can get quite hot.

✿ While the onions, garlic and spices sauté gently, peel and cut the squash into 4 cups of small (one inch) chunks. These fairly small squash cubes will cook quicker in the chicken stock. You can also roast or steam the squash in advance and scoop out the innards if this is easier for you. Store any extra squash or pumpkin in the freezer for later use.

✿ Add the 4 cups squash to the sautéed mixture and stir. If sticky, carefully add a ¼ cup of water and stir well.

✿ Add 32 ounces of chicken stock or, better yet, add the stock you made and stick the lid on. Bring to a boil and immediately decrease the heat and simmer slowly until the squash is fork tender in about 15-25 minutes.

✿ Remove the pot from the heat and let it cool down so you can handle the pot and soup safely. Remove the bay leaves. If you have an immersion blender, place carefully in cooled down mixture and blend until silky smooth OR pour into a food processor and blend until smooth. Return soup to pot and heat thoroughly.

✿ Ladle into soup bowls. Add a dollop of sour cream or yogurt. Sprinkle with finely sliced carrots, celery and/or parsnips for some color and visual elegance. I like it plain and unadulterated. Enjoy!

44

Hoping to See Garlic Greens in the Spring

It was snowing. It was raining. It was sleeting. It was warm and then cool; downright cold and then warm again. That's winter in Maine.

I decided to check under the mulch of shredded leaves and straw to see how the garlic was fairing. All around the garlic bed there was frost with some ice and snow that clung to the mulchy perimeter and soil. The matted straw was frozen. I knew we had had a mild fall, but I was still surprised to find the ground not frozen at all under this thermal blanket. Due in part to last week's rain (oh what a glorious snowstorm that would have been!) the ground was soaking wet—I sunk a hand down and found mud. I dug around for a garlic clove (brrr!) and did not find a single one. So I kept searching and finally discover a nicely sprouted green sprout still under the earth. Whew! Some of my babies are alive and well and living in their nicely prepared bed which was made for them in October. Others I fear may have rotted due to swamp-like conditions.

Perhaps I am overreacting—after all it is one small section at the end of a pretty-large, raised garlic bed. Maybe I didn't estimate correctly where the garlic was growing and dug in the wrong spot. I do have to say that the sight and feel of all that drenched soil (muck comes to mind) gave me a moment of great contemplation and a dreadful feeling of "what if." What if I don't have a garlic crop? What if the cloves rotted in the ground and no beautiful green tops appear in the spring? What if my beautiful garlic cloves so lovingly placed about four inches into the earth aren't even there anymore? That is a gardener's mighty and frightful nightmare.

I heard of someone north of here who lost his garlic crop a few years ago due to no snow cover (insulation) plus very cold temps that damaged the cloves. Garlic growers add a necessary

thick mulch of shredded leaves, hay or straw over the beds and pray for a good snow fall to try to keep any damage from happening. I have, however, never talked to anyone in Maine who lost garlic to over hydration in the winter. Hopefully the ground will freeze, and the garlic will survive. I planted three beds of garlic and one of shallots. Two of the beds are in drier sections of the garden. Hope is part and parcel of a gardener's life. I have the utmost hope and faith that there will be lovely, dancing garlic greens swaying in an early spring breeze. Fingers crossed, knock on wood.

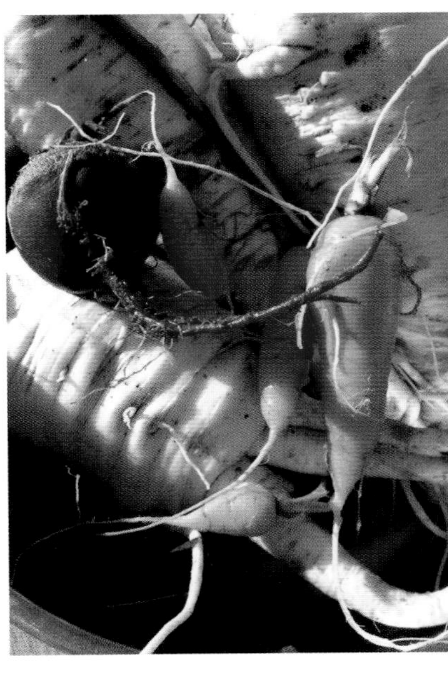

45
Parsnips Become Sweeter with Winter Cold and Frost

What is this long, cream-colored cylindrical root vegetable? Is this a white carrot? Close, but no, this is Pastinaca sativa which can easily be confused as a carrot. This root is known to us as a parsnip. Parsnips are related to carrots and parsley, native to Eurasia and seeds were brought to North America by early immigrants. Parsnips are well known in European culinary circles and pretty popular here in America. The roots store well and can be kept in the ground until spring— root vegetables such as carrots and parsnips are notorious for becoming sweeter with winter frost and deep cold; late winter or even spring harvesting is ideal.

I was introduced to parsnips when I was 19 and living on a Biodynamic farm in upstate New York. I lived with a German family and learned how to prepare numerous dishes that incorporated root vegetables. During the winter months soups, stews, and roasting vegetables kept the kitchen warm as well as body and soul. In the food larder there were onions, garlic, celeriac, potatoes, shallots, carrots, and the beautiful off-white parsnip. Parsnips were cooked, mashed, or added to soups or stews. Even now when I get a whiff of their earthy aroma, it brings back fond memories of this time gone by.

IN THE WINTER

The season for ordering and receiving seeds has come.
The catalogs with pretty pics and written scripts
Have sat around it seems for days, and now are strewn,
Torn and written on, with pages turned and mulled upon.
The human hand and mind
Have chosen what will be in garden, field, protected lee.
The box arrives with packets, all neat and crisp with Latin, drawings, math, and brackets.
Names of plants that grow tall as wheat and others that will complete
This thought, this dream, this planning beam,
That radiates into this gardener's stream.
The stream that flows within my heart and leads to nature, earth, and art.
This garden of gratitude and hope I see,
with thanks to each little seed that sits in packets upon my knee.

People say that parsnips (carrots also) are difficult to grow. The hardest part is getting the seeds to germinate successfully.

Here is some important info to help you grow these roots when Spring rolls round.

Ahh! Certain smells and tastes bring us back to a past moment in our lives. May we cook up some new and joyful memories. May the sweet smell of parsnip, butternut soup or roasted rosemary potatoes, warm your heart, fill your belly and set you up for a Happy Heart-Warming Year Ahead!

✿ Buy new seed from your favorite seed company. Parsnip seeds are considered short-lived and will not germinate well if aged.

✿ Pick a sunny area and prepare a garden row or bed with lots of finished compost. Hand dig or rototill to loosen the soil and compost. Deeply work the soil so the roots can grow more readily. Add any soil amendments such as bone char which is high in the much needed nutrient, phosphorus. By the way, roots crops love phosphorus. Rake, remove sticks and rocks—smooth out the soil.

✿ Sow the carrot seeds—I thickly sow/sprinkle, from my fingertips, the carrot seeds with the grand idea that thinning will always occur when needed. Cover lightly with soil (about ¼-½ inch) and tap down the soil either with your hands or with a rake. This helps keep the seeds from being washed away in a rain. I push each individual parsnip seed into the soil about ½ inch deep and one inch apart.

✿ Be sure to keep the soil moist in the rows or beds where you have planted the seeds. Daily watering may be needed with a hose or can; natural rainfall is the best.

✿ Keep an eye on the soil to check if any seeds have germinated.

✿ Carrots and parsnips can take about 2 to 3 weeks before you see any life in the form of itsy bitsy green seedlings.

✿ Once the seedlings germinate, don't let the soil dry out; you may need to water often but not everyday.

✿ Great thing about parsnips is that the seed is quite large—especially compared to carrot seed—and easy to sow.

✿ Do not save the parsnip seeds for the next year as their germination and viability are fragile.

✿ Another difficulty surrounding parsnips is the actual harvesting of these roots—I had to wrestle them out of the earth with a gardening fork and some muscle! Don't let them get too big as they may become woody in the center and really difficult to pull out. I did have some large roots that ended up being tender, thus edible.

✿ One alert! The leaves of parsnips contain a toxin called furanocoumarin. If the leaves come in contact with your skin, they may leave a rash or blister, so be sure to wear long sleeves when harvesting or thinning. I actually admire and love the leaves—with enough rain they are lush and beautifully shaped. So far, so good. No rashes from the leaves on this gardener's skin.

Parsnips can be steamed, boiled, roasted, grilled, broiled or even eaten raw (haven't tried this). You get the picture—they can be prepared in a variety of ways. I like to steam the roots and

then mash them up with butter, salt and pepper for a nice Christmas dish of smashed/pureed parsnips. Roasting in the oven is my favorite—drizzle olive, avocado or oil of your choice on a variety of washed and dried roots such as carrots, onions, parsnips, garlic and beets—roast at 400 F for about an hour, depending on root size. Sometimes I leave the roots whole or cut the large roots into smaller chunks. Rosemary sprigs can be mixed in with the vegetables. We also tuck parsnips, onions and potatoes in a pan with a roast beef or stick parsnips in a stew or soup. I find them delicious and nutritious providing potassium and fiber to our diets. Hope your experience with parsnips will be favorable.

46

Reaping the Rewards from the Growing Season

This past gardening season was really the very best I have ever experienced as far as growing tomatoes went. A tad dry, but the positive side of that summer drought is that the tomatoes had relatively no blight or fungi spreading on leaves, stems nor fruit. The plants were healthy, and the fruit was abundant, really abundant. I grew Brandywine, Rose de Berne, Sungold cherries, Rutgers and Jet Star plus several other tomatoes.

At the York Farmers Market, I came in second place for the tomato tasting competition. I was "nearly next to" Bill Connelly who won first place in the tomato tasting. I think he has won every year that the tasting has taken place. Bill is known as the lettuce guru—maybe the market will have a lettuce tasting one year.

You ask, why talk about tomatoes in the dead of winter? Well, because harvesting of the tomatoes took place in the late summer early fall and now in winter, my family and I are reaping the rewards of several days of intense labor.

> **A little nurturing, plus a little work at critical times, can reap rewards beyond your wildest imagination. May your work and nurturing provide all that you may need and desire; may any extra spill over to your neighbors.**

Once the tomatoes were ripe they were picked by the basketful, washed, and then blanched in boiling water to remove the skins. After placing in ice water, removing the skins and cutting the large ones in half, the tomatoes were placed on trays and put into the freezer for "flash freezing"—kind of like a mob of fruit all doing the same thing at the same time. After they were frozen solid, the tomatoes were taken out of the freezer, knocked off the pan and vacuum sealed in bags. Steve, my husband, is the main cook. I have tried to "influence" him to leave the skins alone, but he prefers them skinless and whole. He says he can use the tomato in any dish that calls for them and the frozen fruit is especially great in sauces, stews, chili, okra, gumbo, tomato soup, and even on sandwiches. They can be diced, sliced, left in chunks or simmered down into a nice sauce. They are versatile, "taste like summer" and freeze well. Nutritionally, tomatoes offer: lycopene, an antioxidant, vitamin A and C, magnesium and potassium—good for immune and heart health.

So, this next growing season, if you have some extra tomatoes in your garden just throw them in the freezer whole, can them, make salsa or simmer into a sauce. Happy winter as you dream about the first delectable mouthful that you will take in about six months. We have a tradition in which we get on the ground, salt the first tomato and eat the fruit right off the vine!

47
Root Cellars and Winter Vegetable Storage

I once had the opportunity to "visit" a root cellar when I lived in West Virginia. It was built into a small hill and had lots of rock, dirt and sod as insulation. A root cellar is just that—a cellar type structure built into the ground or side of a hill that houses root vegetables. There were many root vegetables such as beets, but what I most remember were the many jars of canned food lined up on the shelves. Before refrigerators there were ice houses and cellars to store food.

When vegetables are harvested from the home, farm or market garden in autumn, storage of the vegetables is vital if you want to reap (eat) your reward over the course of the winter months. You don't want the veggies to freeze or be too warm so that decomposition sets in. Staying alive and not rotting is the goal—a consistent temperature needs to be somewhere between 34 and 40 F with 85% to 95% humidity with good air circulation (fan).

This year I stored butternut, spaghetti and acorn squash, potatoes, onions, shallots, garlic, sweet potatoes and dahlia bulbs in the basement. This has been tricky with the cold spell since the heat had to be up higher to prevent the pipes from freezing which added warmth to the room pushing the temperature up above the favorable storage temperature for vegetables. Dahlias like the temp to be around 35 to 50 F so they seemed quite happy with a little extra heat. Some farms have walk-in coolers to store the turnips, radishes, carrots, and beets with a very steady temperature keeping the roots from getting rubbery.

Over the years I have done the following with storing roots:

✿ I have left the carrots and beets in the ground with mulch covering them for protection. Yes, we have eaten these roots in the winter and with the cold the roots have become sweeter.

✿ Letting a covering of deep snow insulate the carrots and beets has been favorable although that can make them hard to find! Sometimes voles have nibbled on them or the carrots have become rotten.

✿ I have stored carrots and beets in sand in a container in the cellar with moderate success.

✿ I dug a hole or trench in the garden and piled mulch sky high—voles again.

I plan on building a root cellar or small room within the basement to have more control over the temperature and have neat shelves to store apples, onions, carrots, canned goods, etc. I also will try to sink a clean metal garbage can deep into the ground, line with straw and give it a try for storing my root veggies this fall. For now, the radishes, carrots, parsnips, and some beets have been successfully hibernating in the refrigerator in small linen draw string bags made by madder root a made-in-Maine company that designs and sews awesome, functional bags. Homemade muslin bags should do the trick also. I found my vegetables are quite happy as they are cool, but not frozen and have the right humidity. Trimmed beets, turnips and carrots will do fine for a bunch of weeks and maybe even a couple of months just hanging in the refrigerator, not in any sort of bag. Have fun storing your rewards from the garden!

Whether you build your root cellar from old tires, school buses, garbage cans, wood, or earth, may what you store become what you reap!

48
Rosemary Is the Symbol of Remembrance

Rosemary is the symbol of remembrance, friendship, and love, thus it is used in marriage ceremonies. Legend said the flowers turned blue when the Virgin Mary hung her blue cloak on a Rosemary shrub when fleeing Herod's soldiers. Rosemary has been entwined in hair or burned in the home to improve memory, has been made into perfumes and has been grown in gardens for hundreds of years.

This woody, green perennial with pretty pink, white, or blue flowers was not only used to improve memory but it was considered an important medicinal herb used to treat nervous problems, poor circulation, migraines, achy muscles and vertigo. Rosemary has volatile oils, which include borneol and campor and other components such as flavonoids, tannins, rosmarinic acid, diterpenes and rosmaricine. *Rosmarinus officinalis*, now known as

Salvia rosmarinus, is native to the Mediterranean, grows wild in Europe and is grown throughout the world having an upright or prostrate evergreen branch-like appearance—both varieties work well for container planting, hanging baskets as well as out in your herb garden. Rosemary grows great in hardiness zone 8-10, but some varieties such as "Alba" have been known to survive winters in more northern climes. I've seen a large Rosemary growing year-round in a green house in Zone 5. Be sure to have well-drained soil with a pH of about 6.5 to 7.0 and full sun to benefit optimal growth.

Since I live in an area that can get pretty darn cold in the winter and I certainly don't want to lose my rosemary plant to Ol' Man Winter, I dig up the plant each fall and transplant it into a large pot and lug it inside the house (actually I get help from my very strong son). In past years I have unfortunately lost my small indoor rosemary plants to a fungus that covered all the green leaves with a whitish mold which eventually killed the plants. This mold is powdery mildew. My 9-year-old large rosemary plant sits near a sliding glass door so it gets a lot of sun and still

Since rosemary is the herb of love and friendship and remembrance let us sprinkle a good dose of rosemary hither and thither, lest we forget.

remains cool. I do not spray the leaves as is suggested in some gardening books; I water or saturate the roots only one time per week and let the pot dry out in between. This reminds me of the baseball players who don't dare change a thing as they don't want to "jinx" their game—if it is not broken don't fix it—if it is doing well then keep doing what you are doing. I've heard time after time, "move that rosemary plant"—no way!

Personally, I am familiar with the use of rosemary oil to relieve the pain of sore muscles, in shampoos and as an anti-infective. I make a tea using oregano, thyme, rosemary, turmeric, and pepper to ward off a cold or flu virus, add the sprigs to olive oil for a muscle massage rub and an added bonus is the uplifting and lovely aroma. Rosemary sprigs or leaves trimmed off my plant are ingredients in the bone broth or chicken soups; in this house the little branches can be found inside a whole roasted chicken or smothering a pork tenderloin. It tastes great with poultry, fish, lamb, beef, game, with eggs, veggies, soups, marinades, salad dressings, and sauces—whole or ground, fresh or dried it is a popular culinary herb that also has wonderful medicinal, ornamental and cosmetic properties.

Another important feature of this member of the mint family due in part to "secretions" and "scent" is that *Rosmarinus officinalis* is beneficial to other plants. Rosemary repels the carrot worm butterfly, so the carrots aren't bothered by the insect. Rosemary also repels moths and mosquitos. This year the carrot patch will be dotted with small plantings of young rosemary plants (or just take some of their cuttings and place them near the carrot babies) and the woolies will have little fragrant branches interspersed amongst the sweaters. To propagate or grow new rosemary plants use the layering technique which produces roots on a stem that is still attached to the mother plant. You bend a hardy stem near the ground or dirt in the pot, cover it with an inch or so of soil, water, and little roots should grow to produce a new plant. Cut the stem/new plant and replant.

49

Sowing the Seeds of Spring

It is official. The seeds have been sown and the start of the gardening season has truly begun! The onion and shallot seeds have been planted which need a long growing season.

So you want to try starting your own plants, but are not sure how to get started? The following will help you get on your way.

✿ First, gather all your supplies. You will need containers, potting soil, viable seeds, plastic to cover the containers and rubber bands. I ordered my supplies from Fedco: Living Acres Light Mix and Germination Mix and cardboard planters. Johnny's has a good starter mix and many landscaping or gardening businesses do as well. You can also use wooden or plastic trays with lids or peat pots.

✿ Once you have all the necessary items, spread some newspaper or tarp on a flat surface inside your house or on your porch or deck to be used as your working station; cut some newspaper in the shape you need to plug up the holes in the bottom of the containers and fold 2 or 3 times and place over the holes of the fiber paks so the planting medium does not wash away. Then place the soil into the containers about ¾ full or more. I use a quart yogurt container to scoop out the soil; it also pours out well. Onion seeds are large and visible (black) so I shake them out of the seed packet and try to evenly spread them throughout the entire planter. You don't want them too thickly sown as the seedlings may crowd out one another. (I am known for sowing too thickly, not thinning.)

Dirt, warmth, water; life emerging from the dark; a moment in winter to pause and ponder life.

✿ Now you have seeds sitting on top of your planting medium, so cover your onion seeds with about a half-inch of the soil. There are wonderful planting guides in various seed catalogs, online and in gardening books. In the Fedco catalog, you can look up information on hundreds of vegetables, herbs and flowers and gather all kinds of info—number of seeds per ounce, when to start the seeds, seed depth for planting inside in pots and outside for direct sowing in the garden, whether the seeds need light to germinate, days to maturity, the minimum temperature for germination, planting dates, etc.

For example, if you are starting tomatoes inside, you would reference the guide to see when to start them and to find out how much soil should cover the seeds—it would be about ¼-inch to cover tomato seeds. Use a ruler and hold it in the pot, if that would help you. Generally the larger the seeds the more soil you need to cover them. Now gently pat down the soil all over the container then very carefully water the container, with a gentle drip or spray. You want to soak the seeds and soil and be sure the water doesn't "erode" or wash away all your hard work.

It may be winter, but there is a rumbling and a slow beat of the garden drum—a beat that signals the start of another season; a new season of growth and expansion; a season of new beginnings and new endeavors. Let the drum roll begin. Our hearts know that spring is just around the corner with signs of new beginnings here, there, and everywhere! Ol' Man Winter is hanging on to us for a bit but will loosen his grip. Inhale the spring fragrances that will fill our souls with delightful newness.

✿ I cover the pots with plastic wrap, securing it with a rubber band snugly around the top to keep the soil moist until germination. The plastic prevents the soil from drying out. Some people have heat mats to warm the container from the bottom. I place the pots in my furnace room. In about one week little onion plants emerge. Be sure to remove the plastic cover. Instead of plastic, try wax paper to secure over the containers.

✿ Some people have success with seedlings growing on a windowsill. I use full spectrum grow lights until they are ready to get hardened off on the deck or in a cold frame in the garden. I often bring them out in the day with a bit of shade and back inside if it is going to be cold at night.

✿ Something to remember: you would not start tomatoes in January as they would get way too leggy before you could plant them into your home garden in May or June. Timing is everything! Now, if you have a greenhouse that is heated, then by all means get started early.

50

Start in January if You Want Beautiful Lisi in the Summer

Today is a perfect winter day to start some annual flower seeds. The seeds of Lisianthus or Eustoma grandiflorum are being sown inside the house because I do not have a heated greenhouse. Lisi are lovely double petal flowers that resemble roses (no fragrance however), buds streaming down the stems and with layers of petals, makes this a beautiful and very special cut flower. Lisianthus come in many colors: blue, pink, yellow, lime green, apricot, white, and blue picotee. The blooms really are striking in a bouquet and last upwards of two weeks in a vase *and* they withstand cool temps during the autumn months. Lisi take about 150 days to bloom, so this is a long process; the seeds are generally started about 3 months before the last frost in Spring. Folks, it is now start time!

If you follow these directions, you will have a good chance of successfully growing Lisanthus flowers from seed. As with any sowing, whether vegetable or flower, you need to gather all your supplies: containers, soil, or potting medium to support young seedlings, marker, paper, rubber bands, plastic wrap or wax paper and viable seeds.

✿ Mark the containers to identify what you are planting; add the date, name of flower—include any other info you wish. I use cardboard fiber pots to start most of my seedlings and document on the sides with a permanent black marker. Flat wooden markers work well also—place them horizontally on the potting medium until the seedlings emerge and the clear plastic is removed. Just stick them in the side of the pot—just don't let any wee fingers shuffle them about or you won't know which is which until they bloom!

✿ Cover the holes in the bottom of the pot so you don't lose any of the soil. I use unprinted newspaper from a huge roll that I have had for years—you may also use regular printed newspaper, but with no color ink or just use paper towels or a paper bag. I cut the plain paper and fold it, so it is at least double in thickness.

✿ Local garden centers and online companies sell seed starting supplies in all shapes and sizes—peat pots, plastic trays with plastic lids—an array that will surely float your gardener's boat. I order potting soil from Johnny's and Fedco—mix them together in a large stainless steel bowl and use this mixture in the Kord Fiber Paks from Fedco. Today I am using Johnny's 512 "compost based growing medium."

✿ Fill the cardboard fiber garden pak to about 3/4 full or nearly to the top for Lisi and dampen the medium really well. Spray gently until the soil is saturated or gently drip from the faucet.

✿ Lisianthus seeds are very tiny even though they are pelleted with a covering of clay; this makes them bigger and more uniform to plant. I carefully try to drop the seeds uniformly throughout the surface of the wet 512. I do this by rolling them out of the little, hard plastic containers they arrive in. The seeds tend to roll and sometimes bump together on the surface of the potting soil. I use the end of a pen to move them around the pot. Carefully mist them with a spray bottle to get them wet. Lisi need light to germinate so DO NOT cover them with the potting mix. This is very important! Light, water and the right temperature are just what these seeds need.

✿ After getting the seeds damp, I place plastic clingy wrap over the box and secure it tightly with a rubber band. Keeping it snug will help hold in moisture. I wish there was a non-plastic choice such as wax paper, but I have not been successful yet in finding an alternative that really works for me.

✿ You may be able to keep them near a windowsill to germinate, but these seeds need a constant 70 to 75 degree temperature and light to emerge. I put the pots in the furnace room near a window. Checking the temperature by the windowsill or room is a good idea. One must be patient as it takes about 10 to 15 days to see any signs of germination. Once there are seedlings breaking through, I immediately take the plastic off and let the air circulate to prevent any fungi from taking hold. I then stick the pots under grow lights as close to the light as possible—the seedlings may

be 1 inch from the light. The daytime temps, where my table with lights is located, are usually around 70 F. and 60 F. at night. I water the little plants a couple times per week and then weekly when they are taller; check the planting medium daily as you may need to water more often depending on how dry the planting medium becomes. It is a fine balancing act between too much water and not enough water. You can do this!

✿ If your seedlings are getting tall after several sets of leaves have emerged, you can transplant by pricking them out of the soil and carefully planting into single peat pots or other containers. I like leaving them in the box and then transplanting the seedlings right into the garden. The roots have generally grown long and strong at this stage.

✿ The time to plant out the Lisianthus is around late May, after the chance of frost has passed. Check "last frost dates" in your locale for the best time to transplant directly into your garden. The garden soil needs to have wheelbarrows of compost, the plants will need plenty of sun and the soil will need to drain well. If you desire, this would be the time to add organic fertilizers such as fish meal, Azomite, sulfate of potash or kelp meal to provide macro and micro nutrients. Having your soil tested may be a good idea—the pH that Lisianthus like is about 6.5 to 7. With a bucketful of luck, you may be cutting armfuls of Lisi and enjoying them for weeks on end this coming growing season.

51

Summer's Harvest Helps with Winter Baking

This past growing season the pumpkins grew well with no drought or blight affecting them adversely. There were a good number to harvest and even store for winter. The word pumpkin is derived from the Greek word "pepon," which means "large melon;" in French it is "pompon," the British call it "pumpion" and here in the USA we call it pumpkin. I grew four pound pie pumpkins called "New England Pie" (Small Sugar)—little decorative ones named "Jack Be Little" that have heavy ribbing and this year a white pumpkin called "Lumina." The pie and larger pumpkins are taking the place of the butternut squash in various recipes this winter. I love the squash, but unfortunately have eaten most of them; I am so glad the pumpkins did well so I can experiment with these autumn harvested beauties. Butternut squash has always been a favorite as it is most versatile. Many culinary dishes have squash as an ingredient. Examples are soups, stews, mashed dishes, pies and desserts.

The pie pumpkins are orange in color and *Lumina* or *Cucurbita maxima* are ivory or white—both pumpkins can be carved or painted. The white pumpkins are beautiful in the garden, placed by the front door and work well in your oven. To my delight the flesh is light yellow, sweet and smooth. I baked the two varieties whole and alongside of each other until fork tender. After cutting into the New England Pie, I found it to be fairly stringy, which when puréed still worked great for pie or soup. The *Lumina* was amazingly smooth and looked like it was puréed already! It was made into a puréed soup that also had sautéed onion and garlic, bay leaves (removed before pureeing mind you), cumin, nutmeg, cardamom, cayenne, chicken broth, salt and pepper.

Here is my recipe for pumpkin pie:

✿ Bake whatever pie pumpkin you have, whether white or orange, little or big, round or long. I cut them in half from end to end through the poles, scoop out seeds and strings, then place cut side down in a pan of water and bake at about 375 F until fork tender. Recently I placed the whole washed and stemless pumpkin in the oven and baked it until fork tender, then cut and separated the seeds from the pulp. If you have any difficulty wielding a knife and wrestling with a pepin, then this is the technique you would want to use—wash and toss it in the oven. (Beware when scooping out the pulp as you do not want to add any seeds to the dish.) Seeds however can be cleaned and roasted in a separate pan in the oven, stored and eaten. Steaming the cut halves in a large pot is another way to cook the pumpkin pulp.

✿ I grind (in a food processor or with a rolling pin) 1.5 to 2 cups organic pecans, add a tablespoon of maple syrup, a little nutmeg and/or cinnamon, three tablespoons melted butter and sometimes a teaspoon of vanilla. This mixture is patted into a buttered pie pan of your choosing. Bake at 350 F until slightly brown—watch the pie shell carefully. You can also lay a layer of whole pecans on the buttered pie pan if you don't want to mess with the above ingredients. Wheat free for those who may be inclined.

> Whether you cut the pumpkin end to end or throw it whole in the oven to bake, we are all on a similar path to the finish line. May we all tread that path well, respect the other techniques, enjoy the finished product and share with those who would like a bite.
> Happy Winter!

✿ Rinse the food processor and add 3 cups of pumpkin puréed, 3 to 4 eggs, 1 to 1.5 cups of raw cream, three tablespoons cinnamon, 1/2 to 1 teaspoon of nutmeg, ginger, cloves, cardamom, 1/2 teaspoon sea salt, 1/2 cup maple syrup, more or less of spices and sweeter depending on your taste buds. Sometimes I add a little molasses (about 1 to 2 Tbsp.) which darkens the pie, so go easy—plus it is sweet so add a little—one half tablespoon at a time.

✿ Blend well and pour into the cooled pecan pie crust; bake at 425 F for 15 minutes then turn down to 350 F for about 50 minutes or until the toothpick comes out clean from the middle of the pie. Cool on a rack. I especially like the spicy flavor the next day—cold from the fridge for breakfast.

✿ I love baking pies and making soup from my home-grown squash and this year in particular, pumpkins. If you have never done this, give it a try, as it will be very rewarding and nutritious.

ACKNOWLEDGMENTS

Thanks to my elder brother, Jack, for some manuscript advice and his wife, Anne, who are tyring to make their gardens better.

Profound gratitude to my mother, Beverly, who had been my biggest fan. She always loved my flowers and had been cheering me on mostly via FaceTime.

My Dad, who has departed this earth, loved my Ailsa Craig onions and would eat them like an apple. Thanks for sparking my interest in nature Huck.

Thank you to my sister, Chris, who was there when my mother needed her. My deepest gratitude for all the work she did and does in this caring realm.

My husband, Steve, has kept me very well fed and I thank you for your rock solid and creative cooking skills. I am thankful for each and every delicious and nutritious meal. I am also grateful for all your skills that pertain to wood—nearly anything wooden that is in the garden, such as a raised bed, trellis, or tomato stake, traveled through your woodshop.

Jon, AKA King Kyote, you make my heart sing when I watch you and your gardening skills come alive.

TTori Rasche of Tori Rasche Fine Art and Amy Clark of Ocean Fire Pottery, who knew about the book nearly before anyone else: thanks for putting up with my antics of collaborative art shows, book ideas, overenthusiasm (!) and more.

Karen McElmurry, owner of Simply Grown Farm, who gives me space to vent about drought, cut worms and flea beetles as we commiserate *and* celebrate with each other. Thank you!

To all my gardener friends from New York, West Virginia, New Hampshire, and Maine: I appreciate your ideas, expertise, and learning opportunities. To those who embrace organic and biodynamic gardening, as this may be one of the few approaches to heal our precious and fragile earth. We are all in this together, in one way or another.

To the people who, over the years, have enjoyed my flowers and vegetables, a shout out to each of you.

Michael Steere, my editor. We had numerous delays, but "God willing and the creek don't rise," this book will be thankfully birthed with fiddles playing and stomping feet.

Dear Emily, thank you for reminding me of my taproot, tendrils, and rhizome weaving that is part of my life's work. The woven threads are alive with vitality, love, creativity, and clarity. Thanks for reminding me about the true meanings of life, the importance of being here now and for getting me back on track with the certified health coaching class at IIN and basically back to the herbs.

Mother Earth. You are amazing. You gave me my footing. With help from the angels came strength, courage, lucidity, love and hopefully wisdom! I will do everything in my power to protect you and I remain awe struck by the unfurling of a bean seed: the migrating birds, fish that return to a specific spot to spawn, the rhythms of the tides, the magic and practicality of the bees. Look. Deep. You and I may see and learn much, much more.